Endorsements for
Pathways To Inner Peace

When so much around us gives rise to stress, anxiety, and uncertainty, in **Pathways to Inner Peace**, Diane Dreher offers a gentle yet powerful reminder: we have agency. Through simple, actionable steps, this book shows us how to reclaim a sense of purpose, calm, and hope—one intentional choice at a time. Everything Diane shares aligns with what I know to be true of Hope. Her words are a gift to a world that needs them now more than ever.

Kathryn Goetzke, author, *The Biggest Little Book About Hope*, and founder, the Shine Hope Company.

"I keep hearing people say that we need hope now, more than ever. **Pathways to Inner Peace** offers practical guidance for how to tap not only into hope, but also community, kindness, joy, and so much more. Combining ancient wisdom with cutting edge research in positive psychology, Dreher offers readers valuable insights for achieving a great sense of inner peace, even in troubled times."

David B.Feldman, Ph.D., clinical psychologist, international hope researcher, and author of *Supersurvivors: The Surprising Link between Suffering and Success.*

"*Pathways to Inner Peace* is a vitally necessary book for all who seek deeper connection with themselves, others, and their communities. Dr. Dreher explains 9 specific pathways culled from current research, while guiding readers on how to practice them in daily moments. Transform stress to ease and chaos to calm with the insights and inspiration in this beautifully crafted book."

Gloria DeGaetano, Founder, Parent Coaching Institute

"*Pathways to Inner Peace* bridges ancient philosophy with modern research to offer practical routes to wellbeing and flourishing, even during troubled times. It is a reminder that character and community matter in building a brighter world."

Claire Higgins, Chief Operating Officer / Director of Research & Education, Positive Psychology Guild

"We live in a world today that is volatile, uncertain, complex and ambiguous. Diane's latest book, *Pathways to Inner Peace,* comes to the rescue just in time with her simple yet profound message of hope. Weaving spiritual traditions with modern positive psychology, she will help you to rewire your brain and refire your soul on her beautifully designed path of faith not fear, joy not depression, hope not despair, love not hate. This stuff really works! How do I know? Because I use it daily with my teaching, writing, leadership and mentoring. And you should too!"

Jerry Lynch, Ph.D., Founder of Way of Champions
and author of *Lead with Love.*

"Diane Dreher's ***Pathways to Inner Peace*** is a treasure. Delivering on its title, Dreher's book integrates spiritual traditions with up-to-date scientific research and gives us tools to feel more connected and hopeful in a world that seems to be falling apart. If you've felt stressed, lonely or even mildly hopeless, this book will pick you up and guide you to a path of peace, connection, and wellbeing"

Meg Van Deusen, Ph.D.m Psychologist and author of *Stressed in the U.S.: 12 Tools to Tackle Anxiety, Loneliness, Tech-Addiction and More*

Pathways to Inner Peace is a critically important book at a critically important time. With so many challenges in our contemporary world it is easy to become unmoored, lost, or at least discouraged and discombobulated. Dr. Dreher's new book comes after a series of her other helpful, practical, easy to engage books that direct the reader to find a more satisfying life path. This is a must read and I'll certainly encourage my students and patients alike to read it as it will surely improve their lives...and yours.

Thomas G. Plante, Ph.D., ABPP, *Augustin Cardinal Bea, S.J. University Professor, Santa Clara University,* Emeritus Adjunct Professor in Psychiatry, Stanford University School of Medicine, author of *Living Better with Spiritually Based Strategies that Work.*

"An academic, spiritual - yet practical literary trichotomy of insightful, thought-provoking concepts. It bridges the gap between ancient wisdom and practical application. Diane writes with compassion, simplicity and humility - three jewels of wisdom! A recommended read within times of peace and times of trouble!"

Reece Coker, President of the Positive Psychology Guild, Fellow of the Royal Society for Public Health, Honorary Senior Lecturer at Manchester University.

Pathways to Inner Peace

Finding Connection, Inspiration, and Renewal in Challenging Times

Diane Dreher

For information, contact

MSI Press, LLC, 1760-F Airline Hwy #203, Hollister, CA 95023

Copyeditor: Betty Lou Leaver

Cover design & layout: Opeyemi Ikuborije

Permissions:

Dreher, D. E. (2015). © Leading with Compassion: A Moral Compass for Our Time. In T. G. Plante (Ed.). *The psychology of compassion and cruelty: Understanding the emotional, spiritual, and religious influences* (pp. 73-87). Santa Barbara, CA: ABC-CLIO by permission of Bloomsbury Publishing Plc.

Eknath Easwaran. Excerpts from *Passage Meditation – A Complete Spiritual Practice* by Eknath Easwaran (Nilgiri Press, 4th ed., 2016) and *The Mantram Handbook: A Practical Guide for Choosing Your Mantram & Calming Your Mind* (5th ed., 2008.) Used with permission.

Quote from *Mindfulness for Beginners* © 2016 Jon Kabat-Zinn, used with permission from the publisher, Sounds True Inc.

Kristin Neff, Self-Compassion Break, described in her book, Neff, K. (2011). *Self-compassion: Stop beating yourself up and leave insecurity behind.* New York, NY: William Morrow and cited on her website https://self-compassion.org/self-compassion-practices/. Used with permission of Kristin Neff, Ph.D.

The Quick Coherence® Technique, described on page 82 of Childre, D., Martin, H., Rozman, D., & McCraty, R. (2016). *Heart Intelligence: Connecting with the Intuitive Wisdom of the Heart.* Waterfront Press. The HeartMath Institute grants limited and non-transferrable permission for Diane Dreher to use the Quick Coherence® Technique, in her book titled *"Pathways to Inner Peace."*

ISBN: 978-1-957354-81-1

Library of Congress Control Number: 2025940041

Dedication

This book is dedicated with great love and respect

to Robert Numan, my partner in life and a continuing inspiration.

CONTENTS

Introduction

If you've been longing for a deeper sense of connection, you're not alone. We are living in challenging times. Years of rapid change, the COVID pandemic, natural disasters, and political uncertainty have disrupted our lives. Many of us have lost loved ones, connections with friends and colleagues, familiar routines, and a sense of personal security.

Psychologist Pauline Boss, Ph.D, says that we've suffered "the ultimate loss: the loss of trust in the world as a safe and predictable place" (2022, p. 4; Dreher, 2023). There's an epidemic of loneliness in our world and a dramatic rise in anxiety and depression (Murthy & Chen, 2020; World Health Organization, 2022, 2024).

An increasing sense of loneliness and disconnection has rippled through our world, with disastrous consequences. Research has found that loneliness actually can make us sick (Holt-Lunstad, 2017), and studies have shown that when people feel disconnected, they can become vulnerable to extremism, believing in conspiracy theories and blaming "others" for political problems (Cohen, 2022; Holt-Lunstad, 2017). Much of the current breakdown in our personal and political health can be traced to what Buddhist teacher Sharon Salzberg has called "our delusion of being separated from one another" (1995, p. 1).

Yet, by looking back in time, we can discover a path to hope, for recognizing our disconnection and distress can be the first step on a journey that has inspired spiritual seekers throughout the ages. In the *Divine Comedy,* Dante (c.1321/1955) wrote that "Midway through the journey of my life, I found myself lost and alone, wandering in a dark wood," as he began his journey from loss and separation to connection with the Divine.

This search for greater connection echoes through many spiritual traditions. Christian mystics have written about finding union with God in the state of grace. The journey to liberation and the power of loving kindness are central to Jewish teachings. Buddhism teaches that life is suffering until we connect with compassion for all beings, and a major lesson in the *Tao Te Ching* is realizing our oneness with all creation. In the Hindu tradition, this spiritual journey transformed an insecure young lawyer into Mahatma Gandhi whose message inspired multitudes and liberated India. And today, Twelve Step programs help people heal from addictions when they admit that their lives have "become unmanageable" until they connect with a power greater than they are (Alcoholics Anonymous, 1976). All of these traditions focus on the journey from disconnection and distress to a greater sense of connection, inspiration, and hope, a journey you can begin in this book.

Perhaps you, too, have felt like Dante, lost and confused by life's challenges, searching for greater peace of mind. I know that I have.

I discovered the pathways for this book while struggling with a series of personal losses. First, my parents died, and then I lost my dear friend and mentor, Chris. During COVID, I retired from my faculty position at Santa Clara University, leaving behind my students, colleagues, and the beautiful campus that had been my professional home for years. Then, suddenly, my husband and best friend, Bob, died, and I found myself alone in a house that had once felt so much like home. I was still surrounded by Bob's books, the saddles from his favorite horse, and photos of us in happier times. But now my only daily companion was my little dog, Ginny.

With the familiar foundations of my life stripped away, I began my personal search for connection and peace of mind.

I've always been a seeker, perhaps because I grew up following my Air Force father on his assignments across the country and around the world. Through the years, I've explored many cultural and spiritual traditions.

Raised as a Catholic, I began studying Eastern philosophy and practicing Buddhist meditation, then learned about Judaism from Bob. I did research on Renaissance spiritual poetry and wrote three books on Taoism, finding the light of inspiration in many spiritual teachings.

As I was growing up, whenever my father was transferred to a new assignment, I'd find my way to the local library, discovering books that opened doors to other worlds. In college, I majored in English and went on to get a Ph.D in English at UCLA. Then, I moved to northern California to teach Renaissance literature at beautiful Santa Clara University where I met Bob, who taught psychology and neuroscience. We became partners in life, sharing love, laughter, and campus politics, supporting each other in our research, and exploring the world together. I became so intrigued by psychology that I took night classes to earn a master's degree in counseling. Then, I began doing research in positive psychology, combining psychology and literature in my classes, and becoming a positive psychology coach.

While struggling with loss and searching for greater peace of mind, I drew upon what I'd learned in counseling and my lifelong study of literature and philosophy, reflected in my book, *The Tao of Inner Peace.* However, I soon realized that when darkness clouds our days, we need practical tools to dispel the darkness and reveal the light. I'd begun discovering these tools in positive psychology research conducted with my friend, psychologist David Feldman, Ph.D. In our study, we found how short, strategic steps can build our hope. Acknowledging the power of this approach, our research (Feldman & Dreher, 2012) has been included in over 500 published studies worldwide. As my search for peace of mind continued, I discovered nine powerful pathways to greater connection and inner peace. These pathways have been practiced through centuries of spiritual traditions and described by poets and philosophers. Now they're supported by the latest scientific research.

Although you and I may often *feel* disconnected, scientists have confirmed our essential connection with all creation. Responding with wonder to the beauty and grandeur of the cosmos, astrophysicist Carl Sagan (1980) realized that we are composed of the very elements of the stars. Astronaut Edgar Mitchell

(2008) felt a deep connection to the universe when he looked down through the vast blackness of space at the small blue planet we call home. And the 2022 Nobel Prize in Physics was awarded for research that demonstrates our intrinsic interconnectedness, revealing how subatomic particles can behave as one, even at great distances.

Albert Einstein realized that we are each an intrinsic part of the universe. When we feel disconnected, he called this an "optical delusion of consciousness." The path to peace of mind, he maintained, involves transcending this delusion of separation (1950, p. 206).

Helping you free yourself from this sense of separateness, *Pathways to Inner Peace* can become a spiritual guidebook on your own journey to greater peace of mind.

You will not travel this journey alone for this is a pilgrimage we will take together in an ongoing conversation about our hopes, our fears, and what matters most to us. I will share stories of my own struggles and spiritual adventures along with those of my friends, favorite writers, and others who have taken this journey before us. As you read our stories, you may find yourself recalling your own stories of struggles with uncertainty as well as times when you felt a deep sense of connection and transcendence, recognizing that on this journey of oneness, we are all connected.

Research has shown that we can make our journey of connection through many pathways, including meditation, relationships, and inspiration from nature and the arts. As you make your way through this book, you'll be exploring these nine pathways to inner peace:

1. **The Path of Mindful Presence.** We often feel disconnected because we're not fully present with what we're doing. Studies have shown that most of us spend much of our time rushing, multitasking, and doing one thing while thinking about something else. The practices in this chapter can help you feel more connected by bringing your attention back to the present moment.

2. **The Path of Nature.** For centuries, poets and philosophers have recognized our intrinsic connection with nature. Now research has shown that by connecting with nature we can transcend feelings of separation and gain greater peace of mind, vitality, and hope. The practices in this chapter can help you reconnect with this healing power of nature for yourself.

3. **The Path of Community.** We all need a sense of belonging, to feel at home in our community and our world. Yet, lately many of us have been feeling lonely and isolated. The practices in this chapter will show you how to cultivate a stronger sense of community from your close relationships to your neighborhood, workplace, and beyond.

4. **The Path of Meditation.** For centuries, meditation has been a source of inner peace. Now research shows that meditation can relieve anxiety, lower our blood pressure, reduce inflammation, and strengthen our immune systems while also reducing feelings of loneliness and isolation. This chapter will introduce you to a range of simple meditative practices to cultivate inner peace.

5. **The Path of Kindness.** Kindness, which the Buddhists call compassion, can bring us greater peace of mind and connect us to all living things. This chapter will offer practices to help you develop greater kindness for yourself and those around you.

6. **The Path of Purpose.** Becoming overwhelmed by our daily duties, demands and obligations can disconnect us from a deeper sense of purpose. Research has shown that developing a sense of purpose can bring us meaningful connections and a greater sense of hope. The practices in this chapter can help you connect with a greater sense of purpose in your own life.

7. **The Path of Intuition and Inspiration.** If you've ever had a flash of insight or experienced a remarkable coincidence, you've connected with the power of your intuition. This chapter will show you how

to reach beyond surface awareness to connect more often with your intuitive wisdom and guidance.

8. **The Path of the Arts.** For centuries, the arts have offered a source of inspiration that can touch our hearts and transform our lives. In this chapter, you'll learn how to find greater connection, joy, and meaning through enjoying music, literature, dramatic art, the visual arts, and by creating your own artwork as well.

9. **The Path of Joy.** For many of us, it's been hard to feel positive lately. In recent years, our lives have been turned upside down by the COVID pandemic, political conflicts, natural disasters, economic uncertainty, lost relationships, and heartbreaking wars around the world. Yet, research shows that even during troubled times, moments of joy can bring us greater meaning, resilience, healing, and hope. The practices in this chapter can help you discover how, when your heart expands in joy, you'll find light in the darkness and realize your deep connection to the beauty of life.

All of these pathways have been validated by research in psychology and neuroscience, demonstrating how they can make a positive difference in our lives.

As you make your way through this book, you'll find that some pathways appeal to you more than others. You may find greater connection through nature, the arts, or cultivating community. And within the nine pathways, some practices may bring you a joyous sense of connection while others may not. This is normal for we are all individuals. I invite you to see this process as a personal experiment, an ongoing journey of discovery.

How to Use This Book

This book has been designed as a nine-week journey through the nine pathways to inner peace, offering an active practice for each day of the week to bring greater connection and hope to your life. Research (Feldman &

Dreher, 2012; Snyder, 1994) has shown that cultivating hope involves both awareness and positive action.

Some people may prefer to read the entire chapter for each pathway first before beginning the daily practices. Others may take more than a week to make their way through each pathway. To move forward on your journey, I encourage you to find a way that works best for you.

However you proceed, you'll find that each chapter begins with an introduction to the current pathway where you'll discover insights from spiritual traditions and current scientific research. You'll then be asked to set an intention for your journey through this pathway. Each of the next five days will offer you a new practice to include in your activities. At the end of each day, you'll be asked to reflect on that practice—what you did, what you experienced, and what you learned. If you choose, you can also preview the next practice to plan for the day ahead. On the seventh day, you'll be invited to reflect on your experiences and choose a favorite practice to take with you on your continuing journey to inner peace.

Each pathway may take you more than a week to complete. Our daily schedules differ and even with the best of plans, life happens. If you miss a day or two, just go back to your pathway and pick up with the next practice. Don't let small interruptions throw you off course. The important thing is to keep moving forward. The journey to inner peace is about excellence, not perfection.

To track your progress on the journey, I encourage you to record your insights. You may want to keep a journal. Or you can write your thoughts in the space for notes at the end of each chapter.

You can take this journey as a personal spiritual practice. Or you could decide to read this book with a friend, taking the journey together and sharing your reflections and insights. Some people may choose to form "connection circles," working through the pathways on their own, then meeting in small groups each week to share their discoveries on the journey.

Once you make your way through this book, you can choose some of your favorite practices to include as a regular part of your life. Whenever you find yourself feeling down, you could open this book at random to find a practice that will help light your way.

Your small steps on these pathways will add up, for research has shown that consistent effort over time can make a major difference in our lives. A UCLA study (Schwartz, 1998) revealed that when people practiced a simple mindfulness exercise for only ten weeks, they experienced not only greater peace of mind but actual physical changes in their brains. Similarly, during your journey through these pathways, the practices in this book could change your life in surprising and remarkable ways.

The pathways we'll be exploring together have brought me greater connection, joy, and inner peace. I recommend them to my clients because I know what a difference they can make in our lives. As you join me for the next few weeks, you'll begin your own transformational journey. And as we walk this path together, you may discover a powerful source of inspiration to light up the dark corners of your life with greater joy, hope, and inspiration.

Welcome to the journey of a lifetime.

CHAPTER 1

The Path of Mindful Presence

PREPARATION
WEEK 1, DAY 1

One reason we can feel so disconnected and distressed is that we're often not present with what we're doing. Research (Killingsworth & Gilbert, 2010) has found that nearly 50% of the time most of us are doing one thing while thinking about something else. Does this sound familiar?

Let's imagine that it's Monday morning. Your alarm goes off, and you wake up thinking about everything you have to do today. You're caught up in planning, worrying about the report you're giving at work and everything that could go wrong. You get up, head for the bathroom, brush your teeth, and splash cold water on your face. Then, you go to the kitchen to make coffee. Sitting by the window with your phone, you scroll through your email, barely tasting your coffee as you deal with announcements, ads, and questions. Suddenly, you realize you're running late. With no time for breakfast, you rush to get dressed and head out the door. Halfway to work, you realize you've left your report on the kitchen table.

Obsessive planning, worrying, multitasking, and rushing can keep us from being present. Let's begin the day once more with a sense of presence.

It's Monday morning. When your alarm goes off, you pause to take a deep breath, feeling the comforting warmth of your blankets. Then, you get up, noticing the sunlight shining through your bedroom window. Opening the shades, you look out at the trees and the bright blue sky. With a sense of gratitude, you wash, dress, and head for the kitchen where you put on the coffee and cook a bowl of oatmeal in the microwave. Sitting by the kitchen window, you savor your coffee and breakfast, smiling when you see the sparrow at the bird feeder outside. Clearing up the breakfast dishes, you pick up your report and head out the door on your way to work.

What makes the difference between these two mornings? Attention. We live life on two levels: our separate self and our connected self. On one level, we are all individuals, with our own names, strengths, and personal histories. Yet if we live *only* as our separate selves, we can become disconnected. We can see life as a struggle, spending most of our time planning, worrying, and craving external approval. When we expand our attention beyond our separate selves, we can recognize our oneness with all creation, opening our hearts to a more inspired and holistic view of life.

Psychologist Peter Levine, Ph.D., (2008) has found that trauma involves a loss of connection—with our bodies, ourselves, other people, and our world. But even if we don't suffer from trauma, neuroscience research has found that we can spend much of our time living in the *default mode network,* the chain of thoughts and inner chatter that reinforces our separate self. At best, this network enables us to function as individuals, planning, and achieving our goals. But when we become too focused on ourselves, this network can disconnect us from others and lead to obsessive worry, anxiety, and depression (Hamilton et al., 2015).

The Buddhists teach that attachment causes suffering—attachment to ourselves that disconnects us from the present moment and the world around us. And today's many distractions focus our attention on our separate selves— information overload from the news, email, social media, and advertising; external demands; and deadlines. Ours is a culture of distraction. I heard a recent ad on the radio saying that the San Francisco Giants' Oracle Park is the first baseball park in the country with Wi-Fi so fans can "stay connected" while watching the game—connected to their phones, checking messages, email, and social media, while disconnected from the game itself. In our distracted lives, many of us do too many things at once and rush from one commitment to the next, ruminating about the past or worrying about the future.

Confirming age-old Buddhist teachings, today's research has found the solution. We can become more mindful, awakening to the present moment, to the wonder and possibilities of our lives. Psychologist Lisa Miller, Ph.D., (2021) has found that with a mindful, "awakened brain," we feel more at peace and at home in the world. By becoming more mindful, we can move from disconnection to connection, from frustration to compassion, opening our hearts to trust in life's unfolding journey.

Declaring his independence from mindless distractions as he began his own journey of awakening, Henry David Thoreau moved into his cabin at Walden Pond on Independence Day, July 4, 1845. In his journal, he asked himself, "What kind of gift is life unless we have spirits to enjoy it and taste its true flavor?" (Stapleton, 1960, p. 165). In his classic, *Walden,* he wrote, "I went to the woods because I wished to live deliberately" (Thoreau, 1960, p. 72). For us today, to "live deliberately" means paying attention to the present moment, living more mindfully, and becoming more aware of the precious gift of life.

There are thousands of studies on the healing effects of mindfulness. Research has shown that mindfulness-based interventions can relieve stress, anxiety, and depression along with a range of physical diseases (Shapiro & Carlson, 2009). Mindfulness can also help alleviate loneliness and strengthen our sense of connection with others and our world (Teoh et al., 2021).

This chapter will help you build your own sense of connection by first identifying three common distractions— (1) compulsive planning, (2) multitasking, and (3) hurry—and then showing you how to overcome them with mindful practices.

1. Compulsive Planning. As you know, we spend nearly half our time doing one thing while thinking about something else. Unless we consciously focus our attention, a nonstop rush of thoughts drones on in our heads like the constant chatter on a talk radio station. Even when we're listening to someone else, this inner dialogue will rehearse our answers or rush us into future planning. Research shows that such a disconnected mind is a stressed mind (Killingsworth & Gilbert, 2010).

Beneath all the incessant planning is often fear of helplessness and losing control.

The fact is that we cannot control everything in life, including the weather, the news, and other people. In a way, life is like a tennis game. We can set our intention and serve the ball but cannot control how the other side responds. We can only be present, ready and resilient when the ball comes our way again. And the more present we are, the more effective our response is.

Research has found that there's a big difference between worry and problem solving. When we're stuck in worry, our bodies and minds react with ongoing stress, which actually limits our ability to think clearly and discover effective solutions (LeDoux, 1996). Excessive worry and rumination can also drag us into a downward spiral of helplessness and depression (Williams et al, 2007).

If you've been struggling with anxious and depressed feelings, you may need to reach out to a supportive friend, counselor, or therapist. But often, paying mindful attention to how you feel can relieve your stress, moving you from compulsive planning and worry to greater clarity and peace of mind.

2. Multitasking. Multitasking, trying to do too many things at once, splits our concentration and distracts us from the present moment. One evening when I was in graduate school, I made myself a special dinner, carefully slicing carrots, onions, and tofu, then stir-frying them with snow peas and bean sprouts. I added a little soy sauce and served my creation over brown rice in my favorite porcelain bowl. Putting an album on the stereo, I sat down to enjoy my dinner. But then I began worrying about my dissertation research. A few minutes later, I looked down at the bowl, and the food was gone. I hadn't tasted a bite. Then from the stereo, I heard the Rolling Stones' song, *You Can't Always Get What You Want.*

You can't get what you want if you're not present to life, if you let multitasking hijack your attention. As Thoreau realized many years ago, "Our life is frittered away with detail." (1960, p. 73).

These days we have distracting details from electronic devices that Thoreau never dreamed of. When I turn on my cell phone (I refuse to call it a "smart" phone), red icons announce "breaking news"—often only celebrity gossip. Advertisements interrupt television programs to sell their products. With cell phones and computers, our workdays can expand to 24/7. And instead of honoring our human nature, we multitask, imitating computers that can have many windows open at once.

My students would tell me how they study while watching YouTube videos and checking social media. I saw this for myself a few years ago when I was a grad student in counseling psychology. In a class on abnormal psychology, I sat in the second row, taking notes on the lecture while I could see the laptops of students in the front row. They were answering email, checking social media, and even watching a hockey game while the professor stood at the lectern, trying his best to teach us about Post Traumatic Stress Disorder.

We cannot multitask without losing focus, without losing connection to ourselves and one another. We miss so much in our lives when we try to multitask.

There's a beautiful statue in our dining room of a young woman meditating, a gift from Karin Foerde, a talented sculptor and psychology major at Santa Clara University. As an artist, Karin knows the power of focused attention. She went on to graduate school at UCLA, where she studied multitasking, finding that we cannot multitask without compromising our memory (Foerde et al., 2006). As research has shown, we don't really multitask. We shift from one task to another, developing memory lapses in the process (Madore et al., 2020).

3. The Hurry Sickness. Meditation teacher Eknath Easwaran grew up in a rural village in India where the pace of life followed the rhythms of nature. When he arrived in New York City as a Fulbright scholar in the 1960s, he was shocked to see everyone rushing around. Easwaran called this "the hurry sickness" (2016, p. 71).

Now research has shown how constantly rushing can indeed make us sick, putting our bodies into chronic stress, which compromises our health and weakens our memory and cognitive ability (McEwen & Lasley, 2002).

Rushing also disconnects us from others, blocking our compassion. Here's one memorable example (Darley & Batson, 1973; see discussion in Dreher, 2015, p. 75). One December day, students at the Princeton Theological Seminary met with a researcher who assigned them to give a recorded talk in the lab next door. Some students were told to talk about their future careers, others about the parable of the Good Samaritan. The researcher gave each student directions to the lab, then told some of them to hurry because they were running late. One at a time, each student walked to the lab, passing through an alley where a young man sat slumped in a doorway, coughing and groaning. If a student stopped to ask if the young man was OK, he said that he had a respiratory condition and needed to rest after taking his medicine. When some students insisted on taking the young man inside, he went inside and thanked them.

The results were revealing. The subject of the students' speech didn't matter. What made the difference was if they were rushing. When they thought they were running late, the ministerial students were much less willing to help a victim in distress. Ironically, the researchers found that some students actually stepped over the victim while rushing to give their talks on the Good Samaritan.

Since contemporary life so often brings us "the hurry sickness," I decided to begin all my classes with a brief mindfulness meditation to help my students be more present to learn. One day, a conversation with a troubled colleague made me late to class. When I got to the classroom, I looked through the glass door to find one of my students standing up front, leading the class in a mindfulness meditation. I paused at the door, becoming more mindful myself, and opened the door after I heard her say:"…and now gently open your eyes to the present moment, ready to learn and discover together." Seeing how the students had taken the opening meditation to heart and made it their own, I realized, once more, how we are all connected.

This week's daily practices will help you expand your own sense of connection by cultivating greater presence. Like any skill, mindfulness improves with practice, so don't be discouraged if you find your mind wandering as you try this week's practices. When this happens—and it will—just go back and repeat the practice to focus your attention.

But first, I invite you to set your intention for the week.

Exercise: Setting Your Intention

What is your intention for this week? (For example, "My intention is to live in the present moment.")

It's important to write down this intention as an invitation to yourself. You can record it here or in your journal.

My intention is _____

Today's Date

Now take a moment to connect with your intention.

- *Take a deep breath and slowly release it.*
- *Recall a time in your life when you felt a deep sense of presence.*
- *Were you connecting with a friend? Meditating? Experiencing the wonder of nature? Playing a musical instrument or singing in a choir? Something else?*

As you open your heart to greater presence and peace in the days ahead, keep your intention in mind.

Each day this week, you'll find a new mindfulness practice for becoming more present. Try these practices one day at a time, and if one of the practices doesn't appeal to you, just repeat another practice. At the end of the week, as you look back and reflect on your experience, choose a favorite practice to take with you on your continuing journey to inner peace.

TAKING A MINDFUL MOMENT
WEEK 1, DAY 2

We'll begin this week's practices by mindfully bringing our attention to the present moment.

Mindfulness, according to Jon Kabat-Zinn, "is awareness, cultivated by paying attention in a sustained and particular way: on purpose, in the present moment, and non-judgmentally" (2012, p. 1). So much of life can pass us by when we are disconnected from the present moment. Becoming mindfully present is simple, but not easy, especially in our Western world that emphasizes external accomplishments and offers so many distractions.

The present moment embodies the Taoist concept of *wu-wei*—being, not doing. When we're in a state of being, we are present, in touch with our feelings. We're not distracted, not emotionally numb, not driven by stress or feeling disconnected and alone, but present in this moment, connected to the flow of life.

We can become more fully present by focusing on our breathing which connects us to the natural world. With each breath, we exchange energies with the trees and plants around us. They breathe in the carbon dioxide that we breathe out and breathe out the oxygen that we breathe in. Breathing in and breathing out, we are intimately connected to the green world around us.

For centuries, many spiritual traditions have practiced slow, deep breathing to attain inner peace, and now research has shown us why this practice works. Slow, deep breathing stimulates the vagus nerve and activates our parasympathetic nervous system, shifting us from a state of stress, confusion, anxiety, and depression to a state of calm, comfort, clarity, and inner peace (Zaccaro et al., 2018).

There are many forms of mindful breathing. To experience these effects for yourself, find a time and place where you won't be disturbed to focus on your breathing, the natural rhythm that connects you with all of life. First read these simple instructions. Then put down your book and begin the practice.

Exercise: Mindful Breathing

- *Take a slow, deep mindful breath.*
- *Feel the breath flow slowly through your body.*
- *Pause for a few seconds—try a count of three.*

- *Then gradually breathe out, releasing any tension.*

- *Breathing in.*
- *Pausing.*
- *Breathing out.*

Only here, only now.

When your mind starts wandering—and it will—bring your attention back to your breath, slowly

- *Breathing in.*
- *Pausing.*
- *Breathing out.*

Feel the deep comforting presence, the gift of this moment, this life

This short breathing practice is simple, convenient, and always accessible. You can practice it whenever you're feeling restless, bored, or anxious, waiting in line, stuck in traffic, or whenever you need to return to the present moment.

Practice this mindful moment once today. Then record your experience here or in your journal.

****

Mindful Moment Practice: _____

                                           Date

When did you do it?_____

What was your experience?_____

STRESS SKILLS
WEEK 1, DAY 3

Today's practice is a two-step process you can use whenever you're feeling stressed.

Your natural stress reaction can help you survive in an emergency—you can run away from a wild animal or jump out of the way of a speeding car. But most of the time, this stress reaction does not serve you. Problems with work, home repairs, bills, or relationships cannot be solved with the stress reaction of fight, flight, or freeze. If your stress reaction becomes constant, it can tense your muscles, shut down your digestive and immune systems, keep you from thinking clearly, and compromise your physical and emotional health.

The good news is that instead of surrendering to constant stress, you can take charge of your life. By recognizing when you're feeling stressed and responding more mindfully, you can create a new reality for yourself.

Developing your stress skills brings you a greater sense of personal control and is the first key to building greater hope in your life (Goetzke, 2022). With all of today's challenges, I'm grateful that I can now recognize when I'm feeling stressed. My muscles tense up, my heart starts racing, and I feel a sense of urgency. Now, instead of surrendering to a cascade of stress, I can do something about it, shifting from mindlessly reacting to making more mindful choices.

Exercise: Stress Skills

You can develop your stress skills with this two-step process:

1. *First, notice and name what you feel:"tense," "anxious," "nervous," "worried." To name it is to tame it. The simple act of naming a feeling shifts our brain from the amygdala, the brain's alarm center, to the language and speech areas in our brain's left hemisphere. Research has found that unless we dwell on an emotion, it takes only 90 seconds for the chemistry of this emotion to pass through our systems (J.B. Taylor, 2021).*

2. *Next, you can breathe—slowly, intentionally, mindfully. As you now know, research shows that taking a few slow, deep mindful breaths can shift you out of stress into a more balanced state (Balban et al., 2023).*

Neurosurgeon James Doty, MD, (2016) takes three deep mindful breaths to become more centered during challenging brain surgery. If this practice works for complex brain surgery, it can also help you deal with the challenges you face, releasing your tension, relieving your stress, and bringing you back to the present moment so you can feel calmer, think more clearly, and make better decisions on your life's journey.

Practice your stress skills once today. At the end of the day, record your experience here or in your journal.

****

Stress Skills Practice: _____

Date

When did you do it? _____

What was your experience? _____

ONE-POINTED ATTENTION
WEEK 1, DAY 4

Although our busy culture encourages us to multitask, we can return to the present moment with a lesson I learned from meditation teacher, Eknath Easwaran (2016): One-Pointed Attention. This means focusing mindfully on one thing at a time.

Practicing one-pointed attention is an art that can bring us greater connection and harmony in a world that is constantly assaulting us with distractions.

When we focus on what we're doing with one-pointed attention, our food has more flavor, our days have more beauty, and our lives have greater joy and meaning. Each evening, I play Bach's Prelude in C major on the piano, a beautiful exercise in one-pointed attention. When I'm fully present, the effect is harmonious, and I can feel the notes reverberate through my body. When my mind wanders, even for a second, I lose focus and play a wrong note— producing discord instead of harmony.

Exercise: One-Pointed Attention. Whenever you catch your mind wandering away from the present moment, you can practice one-pointed attention by

- *taking a slow, deep, mindful breath;*
- *feeling it flow through your body; and*
- *then slowly exhaling as you return to the here and now.*

Choose a reminder. There are many ways to remind yourself to practice one-pointed attention. During her busy days working for social justice, my friend Gertrude used to reach into her pocket where she kept a favorite button and say silently to herself, "present moment, wonderful moment." Some people wear a rubber band on their wrists. One of my clients wears a special ring. My friend Juan, a poet, professor, and spiritual teacher, wears a Buddhist mala, a beaded bracelet, on his wrist. I often wear a mala next to my watch, to remind me to be present whenever I check the time. There is always time to be present.

Now it's your turn to practice one-pointed attention, choose a reminder, and record your experience here or in your journal.

****

One-Pointed Attention Practice: _____

Date

When did you practice it?_____

What reminder did you choose to remember to practice One-Pointed Attention?

_____

What was your experience?_____

CHOOSING AND USING A MANTRAM
WEEK 1, DAY 5

Another practice to bring us back to the present moment is saying a mantram, a spiritual word or phrase. Years ago, at a Spirituality and Health conference, I heard nurse practitioner Jill Bormann explain how she introduced the mantram at the San Diego Veteran's Hospital. She'd been saying a mantram for years as part of her own spiritual practice. In her research study, she asked the medical staff and patients to choose a word or phrase from their own spiritual traditions, say it silently to themselves while doing routine tasks, and then repeat it whenever they felt stressed.

After six weeks, the busy medical staff members experienced greater presence and peace of mind (Bormann, 2010). But even more remarkably, the combat veterans suffering from PTSD found that a mantram helped them divert their attention from triggering events and let go of negative feelings. They became calmer and even experienced better sleep (Bormann et al., 2013). Bormann sees the mantram as a powerful healing intervention—simple, portable, accessible, with no adverse side effects.

The word *mantram* comes from the Sanskrit words *manas* (mind) and *trai* (to set free), meaning literally to free our minds. In the West, we're more familiar with the word, *mantra*, which now means repeating any motivational phrase. *Mantram* retains its original spiritual meaning.

Exercise: Choosing and Using a Mantram

You can choose a mantram from your own spiritual tradition. Some possibilities are:

Lord Jesus (Christian)

Shalom (Jewish)

Om mane padmi hum (Buddhist)

Allah (Muslim)

There are many more possibilities. Or if you don't relate to any traditional religious word or phrase, meditation teacher Eknath Easwaran says that you might choose Gandhi's mantram, "Rama," which means "joy" (Easwaran, 2008). Or you could find another spiritual phrase that fits you.

Once you've chosen a mantram, practice saying it silently to yourself when you're waiting in line at the bank, taking a walk, or doing routine tasks like washing dishes. You can say the mantram at night to help you drift off peacefully to sleep and repeat it whenever you want to experience greater calm.

Practice using your new mantram at least once today. At the end of the day, write down your experience here or in your journal.

****

Using a Mantram: _____

                          Date

What did you choose as your mantram?_____

When did you use it and what was your experience?_____

_____

TAKING A MINDFUL PAUSE
WEEK 1, DAY 6

Taking a mindful pause throughout our days can help us overcome the constant rushing of the hurry sickness and restore our oneness with the present moment.

Many of us are caught up in a hurry because we cram too many activities into our days. Pausing to reflect at the end of the day and mindfully review the next day's plans can bring us greater perspective. If tomorrow's schedule looks too busy, we can delay, delegate, or delete some tasks to make our day more manageable.

We can also pause throughout the day, taking slow, deep, mindful breaths to become more present. My colleague Andre Delbecq, former dean of Santa Clara's business school, used to encourage busy Silicon Valley CEOs to pause each morning for a mindful moment before getting out of their cars at work in order to be more fully present that day. He'd also remind them to pause at their car doors for another mindful moment at the end of the day to release all the work stress before heading home

When I was teaching at Santa Clara University, I hung a bell on the doorknob inside my office door. This "bell of mindfulness," would remind me to pause for a deep, mindful breath before leaving for class. Then, I began seeing each door as a portal to greater mindfulness. I'd pause to become more present at the door of my classroom, the door of a meeting room, and before opening my car door when leaving to return home at the end of the day.

Sometimes, we can get caught up in stress when we're worried about running late. My friend Carolyn Mitchell used to commute from Oakland on the busy Nimitz freeway to teach at Santa Clara University. When she was stuck in heavy traffic, there was nothing she could do to get there faster. But she could calm her racing heart by taking a deep, mindful breath and telling herself, "I am on God's time." A beautiful affirmation like this can remind us that we are connected to a power greater than we are.

When you catch yourself rushing—to meet a deadline, catch up on errands, make an appointment, or meet someone's expectations, you can take a mindful pause. Perhaps, like Carolyn, you can say an affirmation that reminds you of your part in the larger whole.

Exercise: Taking a Mindful Pause

Now it's your turn to practice taking a mindful pause.

- *Will you pause in the evening to look over the next day's schedule and make any adjustments to prevent mindless rushing?*

- *Will you pause at the door of your car and the beginning and end of each workday?*

- *Will you see each doorway today as a signal to pause and take a deep, mindful breath to become more fully present?*

- *Will you find a way to pause whenever you catch yourself rushing, to say an affirmation to become more fully present?*

- *Will you find another way to make a mindful pause part of your day?*

Now record your experience here or in your journal.

****

Taking a Mindful Pause: _____

                                                        Date

When did you take a mindful pause today? _____

What was your experience? _____

_____

How can you make a mindful pause a regular part of your days?

_____

REFLECT AND REVIEW
WEEK 1, DAY 7

This week, you were invited to try these practices:

1. *Taking a Mindful Moment*

2. *Stress Skills*

3. *One-Pointed Attention*

4. *Using a Mantram*

5. *Taking a Mindful Pause*

As you look back on your week, reflect on your responses. Review how each practice made you feel, and choose at least one practice to take along on your journey to greater peace of mind. Then. write down your experience here or in your journal.

****

Exercise: Week 1 Review

Week 1 Review: _____

Date

What practice would you like to take with you?

_____

What feelings does this practice inspire for you?

_____

How can you use this practice to develop greater peace of mind in the days to come?

_____

CHAPTER 2

The Path of Nature

PREPARATION
WEEK 2, DAY 1

When I was eight years old, I had a remarkable experience. I was climbing the redwood tree by our house on Hamilton Air Force Base in California. Higher and higher I climbed, sheltered by the fragrant evergreen boughs, until I looked down at the red tile roof. High above the house and all my daily chores and parents' expectations, I felt my heart expand in joy, one with the tree, one with the sky. I didn't know it then but in that beautiful tree I was experiencing awe.

We experience awe when we connect with the vast mysteries of life, feeling part of something infinitely greater than ourselves (Keltner, 2023). A major source of awe has always been the beauty and grandeur of nature. Over a hundred years ago, psychologist William James recognized that nature has the "power of awakening such mystical moods" (James, 1985, p. 394.)

Nature has inspired people for centuries. In the Middle Ages, Saint Bonaventure encouraged people to meditate on nature as a pathway to God, and people believed that the color green could touch our hearts and awaken our souls (Dreher, 2001, pp. 9, 11). Renaissance poet Thomas Traherne experienced a sense of oneness with all creation, writing that "You never enjoy the world aright, till the Sea itself floweth in your veins, till you are clothed with the heavens, and crowned with the stars" (Traherne, 1960, p. 14).

Nature's transcendent beauty reminds us that we are not alone, even in our darkest, most challenging times. In a Nazi concentration camp during World War II, Viktor Frankl and his fellow prisoners were sitting on the floor of their hut, exhausted after a grueling day's work. They were eating their meager soup ration when another prisoner rushed in, telling them to come out to see the sunset. As they watched the glowing shades of rose and red, high above the gray huts of the concentration camp, the men stood silent in a moment of awe (Frankl, 1984). Appreciating the beauty of nature brought them inspiration and a new sense of hope.

Recent studies reveal just how much connecting with nature supports our health. When journalist Johann Hari (2018) interviewed social scientists about emotional distress, they told him that a major cause of anxiety and depression is disconnection from nature. A British study found that people who moved to greener areas with parks and trees experienced better mental health than they'd had before the move (Alcock et al., 2014).

In your life today, the beauty of nature can heal you on many levels. If you get caught up in an inner dialogue of worry and negative self-talk, research has found that moments of awe in nature can silence the brain regions that produce self-criticism, anxiety, and depressive rumination (Keltner, 2023). Research (Stellar et al, 2015) has also shown that experiencing awe can improve your physical health as well, significantly reducing inflammation by inspiring feelings of elation and interconnectedness.

The sense of oneness we can experience in nature is *not* an illusion. Nature itself is interconnected. Research has found that plants can sense the energies around them and that trees communicate with each other through their root systems (Hugh, 2020). Although our commercial, post-industrial world tempts us to forget this, we are literally *one* with nature. We breathe in what the green world of trees and plants breathes out, exchanging oxygen and carbon dioxide in an ongoing cycle of giving and receiving that sustains the life on this planet.

Experiencing nature's interconnectedness can bring you a deep sense of comfort, an effect that indigenous peoples have long recognized. Native American author Robin Wall Kimmerer (2015) writes of this sense of comfort in her best-selling book, *Braiding Sweetgrass,* and, centuries ago, in ancient China, Lao Tzu wrote in the *Tao Te Ching* that when we see ourselves as part of nature, we can find ourselves at home in the oneness of life (Dreher, 2000, p. 125).

Henry David Thoreau experienced nature's comfort and companionship in nineteenth-century Massachusetts. On a rainy day in his cabin at Walden Pond, he wrote that "I was suddenly sensible of such sweet and beneficent society in Nature, in the very pattering of the drops, and in every sound and sight around my house, an infinite and unaccountable friendliness" (1960, p. 105).

Perhaps you've felt this sense of comfort and companionship with Nature as well. I experienced it years ago as a first-generation college graduate, feeling anxious and uncertain when I began a challenging Ph.D program at UCLA. Returning from campus at the end of the day, I'd often walk a few blocks from my Santa Monica apartment to visit with the ocean. Standing on a cliff overlooking the blue Pacific, I'd feel a deep sense of comfort as I breathed in the salt sea air and watched the waves rhythmically wash in to shore. The sunlight sparkling on the water was encouraging, the rhythmic waves reassuring. Sometimes, I'd bring my books and study by the ocean. Sitting on the cool grass, I'd read for a while, then look out to connect with the ocean, feeling one with the larger rhythms of life.

Connecting with nature can help us feel more connected to each other as well. Research at the University of California, Berkeley, randomly assigned groups of students to look up at either a tall campus building or a grove of towering Tasmanian eucalyptus trees. The students who looked at the trees experienced awe and became more caring. Then, when all the students saw the researcher intentionally drop a box of pens on the ground as part of the experiment, significantly more of the students who'd experienced awe helped pick up the pens. (Piff et al., 2015).

Spending time in nature can also increase our creativity and mental clarity (Bratman et al., 2012). A group of college students once told me that hiking or backpacking—without their electronic devices—helped them relax, cleared their minds, and increased their awareness. Smiling, they said they'd come back from a hike with a deeper sense of who they are and what they value.

When you connect with nature, you can find welcome relief from stress, anxiety, and depression (Berman et al., 2012; Ulrich et al., 1991). And nature can bring you new insights, new perspectives (Atchley et al., 2012). Centuries ago, Renaissance poets and philosophers encouraged people to discover vital lessons for their lives by meditating on nature (Dreher, 2001).

Recognizing how nature's cycles move through summer, fall, and winter to a springtime of renewal can remind you that you, too, are always growing and evolving. Acknowledging your own personal cycles can bring you greater self-acceptance. We each have our own daily circadian rhythms—some of us are morning people, some of us are night people, and some of us somewhere in between. As daffodils blossom in early spring, tomatoes ripen in summer, and chrysanthemums bloom in autumn, you have your own times of growth and fruition. So, it is unnatural to judge yourself in comparison to others.

Finally, nature offers an abiding source of inspiration. Thoreau wrote how one winter day he cut through the ice of Walden Pond to "open a window under my feet, where, kneeling to drink, I look down into the quiet parlor of the fishes. . .; there a perennial waveless serenity reigns as in the amber twilight sky. . . . Heaven," he realized, "is under our feet as well as over our heads" (1960, pp. 224-225).

There are many ways you can connect with nature. My friends have their own favorite practices. Linda walks with her dog in a local park, Will goes on long hikes, Katherine and I enjoy gardening, and for years, my friend Tracey lived in a cabin in the Santa Cruz Mountains. Before commuting to teach at Santa Clara University, she'd begin each day walking through the redwoods and meditating in what she called her "green cathedral." While I live in town, my house is also encircled by trees—Norfolk pines, redwoods, Japanese maples, bay laurels, and birches. The view outside my window as I write this chapter has become my own "green cathedral."

Connecting with nature has brought me a source of hope as I deal with the current changes and challenges in my life. I love visiting with my garden and walking through the neighborhood or local park, where I feel part of the harmony of life. And at night, when I gaze at the stars, I feel a sense of awe at the beauty and grandeur of the cosmos.

Now it's your turn to discover greater connection with nature. Each day this week, you will find practices to help you connect more closely with the natural world to increase your sense of oneness and peace of mind.

Exercise: Setting Your Intention

I invite you to set your intention for the week. (For example, "My intention is to find greater peace in nature.")

It's important to write down your intention as an invitation to yourself. You can record it here or in your journal.

My intention is _____

Today's date

Now take a moment to connect with your intention.

- *Take a deep breath and slowly release it.*
- *Recall a time in your life when you felt a deep sense of peace and renewal in nature.*
- *Were you walking in the park, gardening, looking up at a tree or the clouds overhead, gazing at the stars, or something else?*
- *Keep that feeling in mind as you open your heart to greater peace in the days ahead.*

Each day this week, you'll find a new practice for connecting with nature. Try these practices one day at a time, and if one practice doesn't work for you, just repeat another practice. At the end of the week, as you look back and reflect on your experience, choose a favorite practice to take with you on your continuing journey to inner peace.

I wish you joy on nature's path.

WINDOW PRACTICE
WEEK 2, DAY 2

We'll begin this week's practices by simply looking out the window.

Each morning, I open the shades of my bedroom window to greet the world outside. Connecting with nature, I pause to look at the sky, the trees, and the changing panorama around me. Comforted by the gentle green embrace of Norfolk pines, bay laurel, and redwoods, I begin my morning meditation and writing practice, filled with gratitude.

Did you know that simply looking out the window at a view of nature could improve your health? Years ago, in a Philadelphia hospital, some patients recovering from abdominal surgery could see trees outside their windows while others looked out at only brown brick walls. The people with the view of trees needed less pain medication, suffered fewer complications, and were discharged sooner than the others, demonstrating how even looking out at nature through a window can restore our health and vitality (Ulrich, 1984).

More recent research has found that when windows in our classrooms or offices offer us a view of nature, we experience greater health, satisfaction, and well-being (Farley & Veitch, 2001). In fact, the color green has even been shown to promote greater creativity (Lichtenfeld et al., 2012).

Exercise: Window Practice

You can experience the restorative effects of nature for yourself with today's simple practice. Take a few moments to:

- *Sit or stand beside a window with a view of nature, looking at the trees and sky. If you don't have a window with a nature view, then look at a picture, poster, or video of nature.*

- *Pause, take a deep breath. As you release it, release any thoughts of busyness or worry.*

- *Breathe slowly and deeply, connecting with the green world of nature.*

- *You may notice the patterns of the trees, the sky, the birds or butterflies, or simply the stillness.*

- *Continue to breathe slowly and deeply as you experience greater peace and renewal.*

When you are ready, return to your usual activities.

Practice this window meditation once today. At the end of the day, record your experience here or in your journal.

****

Window Practice: _____

                            Date

When did you do it?

_____

What was your experience?

_____

WALKING IN NATURE
WEEK 2, DAY 3

Taking a walk in nature can be a wonderful process of discovery. When I lived on Hamilton Air Force Base, I used to go exploring with my best friend Shorty, the boy who lived next door. We'd walk down the hill from our houses and crawl under a fence into a nearby cow pasture. There we'd find sparkling rocks and Indian arrowheads from long ago. Climbing the local hills, we'd look out at the landscape and up at the sky, feeling a sense of connection, oneness, and exhilaration. Years later, my husband, Bob, and

I had our own adventures, hiking around a local lake or in nearby nature preserves, discovering native plants and wildflowers along with a sense of joy and renewal.

After all the rain this year, wildflowers are booming profusely in California. Golden California poppies are blooming all over the hills, along the roadside, and around my neighborhood. Seeing them always makes me smile.

Now research has found how even a brief walk in a natural setting can bring us joy and renewal. A study in Japan revealed that "forest bathing" or *Shinrin-yoku* can restore us to a state of harmony both emotionally and physically. When participants sat in a forest and looked around for 15 minutes, then walked around for another 15 minutes, they experienced lower blood pressure, decreased cortisol levels, greater relaxation, and a more peaceful mood—a remarkable effect in only 30 minutes (Park et al., 2010).

Walking in a natural setting can increase our energy, bringing us greater enthusiasm, joy, and vitality. In another study, American college students were randomly assigned to take a short walk either on a tree-lined path by a river or indoors through a series of hallways on campus. After only 15 minutes, those who'd walked out in nature experienced greater vitality than those who'd walked indoors (Ryan et al, 2010).

Further research has shown that walking in nature can raise our mood, relieve depression, improve our thinking skills, help us reflect on our lives and solve problems more effectively (Berman et al., 2012). Perhaps Shakespeare recognized this centuries ago when he portrayed his characters in *As You Like It* solving their problems and discovering new possibilities in the green world of nature.

You can experience nature's restorative effects yourself with a brief walk outdoors—in your neighborhood, a garden, or nearby park—wherever you can find a peaceful green space.

When you take your walk, remember to slow down. Stop to connect, to look closely, to experience the beauty and mystery of nature. You may even feel a sense of awe.

Exercise: Walking in Nature

To begin:

- *Set aside a time when you won't be rushed.*

- *Travel light. As you head out the door, turn off your phone and leave your busy schedule behind you.*

- *Slow down, breathing slowly and deeply as you notice your surroundings.*

- *Don't think, just be. If you find yourself falling back into thinking and planning, take a deep breath to return to the present moment.*

- *Feel the rhythm of your footsteps and the warmth of the sun or the gentle breeze on your skin.*

- *Focus on the trees, the sky, and the natural world around you.*

- *Notice nature's artistry in the sunlight on the leaves or the patterns of clouds overhead.*

When you are ready, return to your daily activities.

Practice Walking in Nature once today. At the end of the day, record your experience here or in your journal.

****

Walking in Nature: _____

                                        Date

Where did you go?

_____

What did you notice and how did you feel?

_____

GETTING IN TOUCH WITH NATURE
WEEK 2, DAY 4

In our fast-paced lives, when we're caught up in our thoughts and daily activities, many of us lose touch with the natural world and become increasingly disconnected and isolated. With today's practice, you can renew your connection by literally getting back in touch with nature.

Physically connecting with nature and savoring its beauty has been shown to reduce stress, lower fatigue, and bring us greater happiness (Sato et al., 2018). Do you remember what fun you had playing outdoors as a child? I loved doing somersaults on the soft green grass, building tree forts with my friends, and playing hide-and-seek at sunset. But today, many of us have lost touch with our environment. Now children spend hours indoors, staring at screens, and as busy adults we often lose touch with our natural environment.

One way we can begin restoring our bond with nature is by connecting with companion animals. During the Covid pandemic, thousands of people adopted dogs and cats who brought them companionship and comfort. Research has even shown that just petting a dog can lower our blood pressure and strengthen our immune systems (Charnetski et al., 2004).

And more people are recognizing this fact. Today, the counseling center at West Chester University in Pennsylvania uses dogs to help relieve stress among their students. At first, they set up an information table at the student union, staffed by a counselor and Tucker, a golden retriever and certified therapy dog. Students began stopping by to pet, hug, and play with Tucker. The program became so popular that the center staff added a second therapy dog, arranging visits by the dogs each month and throughout finals week. Students love the dogs, saying this experience reduces their stress and is the best part of their day (Daltry & Mehr, 2015).

I stumbled upon a similar student reaction a few years ago when we had a new roof and solar panels installed on our house. All the construction noise made my little dachshund, Ginny, nervous. I couldn't imagine leaving her home alone while I was teaching, so I brought her to class with me.

At first, I was concerned that teaching Shakespeare with a dog in the room would be distracting, but the students seemed happier and more engaged, coming up to pet Ginny and wanting to sit close to her. When we walked across campus, more students would come up and ask, "Can I pet your dog?" Later that term, my student Marcy, who suffered from anxiety attacks, brought her therapy dog, Jack, to my office to introduce him to me. Jack is a little black-and-white terrier who'd welcome Marcy when she returned to her dormitory room, keep her company at night and sit on her lap, licking her face to calm her when she felt distressed.

Do you recall a time when you felt comforted by connecting with a dog or cat?

In addition to connecting with our companion animals, there are other ways to get back in touch with nature. A busy writer I know finds stress relief by stepping outside to touch a tree, and I like to touch the fragrant mint and rosemary plants in my front yard.

Exercise: Getting in Touch with Nature

Just a few moments of focusing on the beauty of nature, breathing in the fragrance of herbs and flowers, touching a tree, or petting a dog or cat can bring you a welcome sense of peace.

Today, you can practice getting in touch with nature by stepping outside to focus on a tree or plant or spending time with your dog or cat.

- *Look up at a tree, notice the leaves of a plant, breathe in the fragrance of roses and herbs. Or gaze into your pet's eyes.*

- *Set your thoughts and cares aside as you become mindfully aware of this connection to the natural world.*

- *Then, reach out and touch the tree or plant. Or engage with your pet. Feel the physical connection.*

- *Notice your experience as you connect to the greater harmony of life.*

When you are ready, return to your usual activities.

Practice Getting in Touch with Nature once today. At the end of the day, record your experience here or in your journal

****

Getting in Touch with Nature Practice: _____

                                                            Date

What did you do?

_____

What was your experience?

_____

GARDENING PRACTICE
WEEK 2, DAY 5

When I was five, we lived near my grandparents in Louisville, Kentucky. I remember how my grandfather would carry me on his shoulders into his garden. As we walked among the rows of tall tomato vines, he'd point out the delicate yellow blossoms that became small green fruit, then turned into ripe red tomatoes. It all seemed magical to me. Then, he'd pick a ripe tomato and we'd go into the kitchen to enjoy the warm, sun-kissed flavor of a tomato, fresh from the vine.

During the Middle Ages and Renaissance, gardening was seen as a spiritual practice. Philosophers, poets, and theologians described the soul as an enclosed garden, encouraging people to meditate on the wonders of creation. Today, research has shown that gardening can bring us greater health and well-being; relieve stress, anxiety, and depression; build our muscles; increase our stamina; and help us think more clearly (Soga et al., 2017). It's great physical exercise and can be a spiritual exercise as well.

Years ago, when Bob and I married and bought our new house, I fell in love with the beautiful garden, lovingly tended by Harold and Betty Johnson, the previous owners. When we moved in, the Johnsons left us a bottle of champagne in the refrigerator and packets of food for the roses. Tending Betty's garden inspired me to write my book, *Inner Gardening* (Dreher, 2001), and through the years, the roses, herbs, and trees have become a vital part of my life. Each day, I spend some time in the garden trimming, weeding, and watching things grow, connecting to nature with a deep sense of joy and gratitude.

Exercise: Gardening Practice

You can connect to nature with your own gardening practice. Here are some possibilities:

- *Grow herbs. You can grow herbs like rosemary, parsley, and basil in pots inside your kitchen window and pinch off a little to enhance your meals. To begin, visit your local garden center and bring home your favorite herb in a small pot. Place it in your kitchen window and water it as needed.*

- *Plant vegetables. If you'd like to take your gardening to the next level, cherry tomatoes can be easily grown in pots in a small space like a patio or apartment balcony. Get a small cherry tomato plant at your local garden center and follow the directions about soil, sun, and water.*

- *Plant flowers. If you prefer to grow flowers, buy your favorite flowering plant at the garden center to enjoy in your yard or in a pot on your porch, patio, or in your window. Ask the garden center staff about the plant's needs and care.*

- *Tend your garden. If you already have plants growing around you, you can just go outside to observe, water and cultivate them, watching them grow. There's always something new happening in the garden.*

Choose one Gardening Practice to begin today.

At the end of the day, record your experience here or in your journal.

****

Gardening Practice: _____

Date

What did you do?

_____

What did you experience?

_____

SEEDS OF HOPE
WEEK 2, DAY 6

Seeds are promises of new life, new possibilities, new hope for the future. When you water them, in a few days they will awaken, and tiny green seedlings will spring to life.

I've always been fascinated by seeds. When I was eleven, living in Grandview, Missouri, I saved some pumpkin seeds from Halloween. That spring, I planted them in my mother's rose garden, planning to make pumpkin pie. When a sprawling pumpkin vine appeared, my mother protested, but my father, who loved pumpkin pie, said to let it be. The vine meandered around the rose bushes until large golden flowers appeared, then small green pumpkins. When the pumpkins ripened, I harvested them to make delicious pumpkin pie.

I still love planting seeds. Each spring I soak seeds overnight in a jar in my kitchen window until they sprout. Then I plant them outside. In early March, I sprout snow peas, then plant them in my garden where they grow from tiny green seedlings into plants that produce white blossoms, and then green pea pods. A few days a week, I can harvest a handful of fresh snow peas for dinner. Later, when the weather is too hot for peas, I grow green beans and tomatoes. The beans grow fast, visibly higher from one day to the next. And they have their own intelligence. In a remarkable process called thigmotropism, their tendrils reach out to grasp and climb up their wooden stakes. Then, they produce abundant green beans for summer meals.

For me, summer would not be the same without the taste of home-grown tomatoes. My friend Pat grows her tomatoes from seed, but I take a short cut, buying tomato plants at the garden store. Because tomatoes love sun, I plant them in the sunniest parts of my yard. I've tried many varieties of tomatoes—Better Boy, Early Girl, Cherokee Purple, Celebrity, and heirloom varieties but my favorite, and the easiest to grow, is Sweet 100, which provides an abundance of small, sweet tomatoes that ripen early and keep producing throughout the season.

Tomatoes, for me, represent life's infinite possibilities. The next time you're slicing a tomato for a salad, take a closer look. Each tomato is filled with an abundance of seeds, and each seed could become a new tomato plant, producing even more tomatoes. Hundreds and hundreds of tomatoes, thousands of seeds. Whenever you feel your life is limited, slice a tomato and look inside to recognize nature's abundant promise.

This year I've planted sunflower seeds around my yard. Sunflowers are heliotropic; they track the sun during the day, turning their heads toward the light. In another beautiful lesson from nature, they remind us to turn toward the light in our lives. Sunflowers are the state flower of Kansas, the national flower of Ukraine, and the international symbol of hope.

This week you can begin sowing seeds of hope in your own life. Think of what you'd like to grow more of—a new creative project, more time with loved ones, healthier meals, regular exercise, time to reflect, time for fun, or something else. Then, literally sprout some seeds and watch them germinate and grow, affirming life's abundant possibilities.

Exercise: Seeds of Hope

Here are some steps to sprout your own seeds:

- *Buy a packet of seeds at the local garden store. Peas and beans are easy to grow.*

- *Put the seeds in a jar with a screen or piece of cloth on top, secured by a rubber band around it to keep the seeds inside. Fill the jar with water and let the seeds soak overnight. Then, pour the water out through the screen or cloth on top, and lay the jar on its side. Or plant your seeds in a small pot filled with potting soil. Set the pot or jar by a sunny window, placed on a tray if you need to protect the surface.*

- *Water your seeds daily. Either water the soil in the pot or refill the jar with water, pour it out through the screen or cloth, and lay the jar back on its side.*

- *In a few days, surprise! The seeds in the jar will sprout, or tiny seedlings will emerge from the soil.*

- *You can then plant them outdoors in the ground or in a larger pot, remembering to water them regularly.*

- *As you watch this new life emerging, reflect on the seeds of possibilities in your own life.*

Begin this practice of sowing your seeds today. When the seeds sprout, finish recording your experience here or in your journal.

****

Seeds of Hope Practice: _____

                        Date Begun   Date Sprouted

- What seeds did you sow?

_____

- How did you feel when they sprouted?

_____

_____

- Anything else you noticed?

_____

_____

REFLECT AND REVIEW
WEEK 2, DAY 7

This week, you were invited to try these practices:

1. Window Practice

2. Walking in Nature

3. Getting in Touch with Nature

4. Gardening Practice

5. Seeds of Hope

As you look back on your week, reflect on your responses, review how each practice made you feel, and choose at least one practice you'd like to take along on your journey to greater peace of mind. Then record your experience here or in your journal.

****

Week 2 Review: _____

Date

What practice would you like to take with you?

_____

What feelings does this practice inspire?

_____

How can you use this practice to develop greater peace of mind in the days to come?

_____

CHAPTER 3

The Path of Community

PREPARATION
WEEK 3, DAY 1

We all need a sense of belonging, to feel at home with the people around us in our community and our world (Samuel, 2022). A remarkable long-term study of health and happiness found that belonging to a supportive, nurturing community is essential to our emotional and physical well-being (Waldinger & Schulz, 2023).

The sense of belonging sustains us throughout life. From our earliest childhood, we need the stability of secure attachment (Bowlby, 1969, 1973, 1980), a warm and predictable relationship with caregivers that provides a solid foundation for our lives. As teenagers, we need a sense of belonging and engagement or we can suffer from chronic stress and anxiety (Challenge Success, 2024). The Harvard longitudinal study of older adults found that the determining factor for living longer, healthier lives is *not* professional or economic success, but a strong sense of belonging (Waldinger & Schulz, 2023).

Research has shown how a sense of belonging can improve our health and change the way we see ourselves and our world. This sense of belonging reduces inflammation and positively affects our brains, offering structural protection against depression (L. Miller, 2021). A loving connection to those around us is an essential key to hope (Goetzke, 2022) and can inspire us with what Buddhist teacher Thich Nhat Hanh (1998) called "interbeing," an awareness that we're part of something larger than ourselves.

Becoming part of a supportive community, even for a short time, can bring us shared resources, collective wisdom, and a heartfelt sense of connection. I learned this years ago while traveling by train through Italy. It was getting late when the people in my compartment learned that the dining car hadn't been connected at the last station. This meant we'd go without dinner. But then something remarkable happened. The German woman and her daughter sitting across from me offered to share their cheese and fruit. The Polish woman beside me offered salami and jar of sparkling strawberry jam. I brought out a loaf of bread, and a young French student shared his bottle of wine. Together, we created a picnic dinner. Sharing food and stories, we became a community. In all my travels, I don't remember a single meal I've eaten in a dining car, but I still recall the joy when five strangers discovered community by sharing our evening meal together.

Yet lately, many of us have lost our sense of belonging. We're spending more time relating to our electronic devices and less time personally relating to the people around us. Psychologist Jean Twenge, Ph.D., (2019) discovered a dramatic increase in loneliness and anxiety among teenagers that coincided with their widespread use of smartphones and social media. The years of isolation during the COVID pandemic have further eroded our circles of personal relationships.

To restore our sense of belonging, we need to *actively* cultivate community. We can begin with what psychologist Pauline Boss, Ph.D. calls our "psychological family," people who love and support us, whether they're actual relatives or a chosen family of friends (personal communication, November 10, 2023; Dreher, 2023).

To strengthen our hope and wellbeing, we also need expanding circles of community, a range of personal connections from these close relationships to informal social ties (Collins et al., 2022). A British study reported on "social prescribing," in which instead of automatically prescribing pharmaceutical drugs, doctors can also prescribe a range of options from self-help groups to volunteer work, book groups, gardening groups, and other opportunities to help people form new social bonds (Brandling & House, 2009).

Even short contacts with other people can strengthen our sense of community. Psychologist Barbara Fredrickson, Ph.D., (2013) has found that casual interactions, a smile or kind word to people we encounter in daily life, from a neighbor, a colleague, or the grocery store clerk, will benefit both the giver and the receiver. These "micro-moments of connectivity" can raise our mood, relieve stress, and reduce inflammation, promoting greater physical and emotional health. These small contacts can create a positive ripple effect, building greater community around us.

As meditation teacher Sylvia Boorstein (2002, p. 9) reminds us, "When we aren't frightened into self-absorption, we look out for each other." When we have a sense of belonging, we care for each other as part of a warm, supportive community that helps us feel more at home in our world.

This week, you can increase your sense of belonging by exploring ways to cultivate greater community in your life, including connecting more intentionally with loved ones, friends, neighbors, and the people you see each day.

Exercise: Setting Your Intention.

It's time to set your intention for this week. (For example, "My intention is to cultivate community in my life.")

It's important to write down your intention as an invitation to yourself. You can record it here or in your journal.

My intention is_____

Today's Date

Take a moment to connect with your intention.

- *Take a deep breath and slowly release it.*
- *Recall a time in your life when you experienced a sense of connection that made you feel seen, loved, and supported. Was it with a friend, family member, mentor, or someone else?*

As you open your heart to greater connection and community in the days ahead, keep this experience in mind.

Each day this week, you'll read about a new practice for cultivating community. Try these practices one day at a time, and if one practice doesn't work for you, just repeat another practice. At the end of the week, as you look back, reflect on your experiences and choose a favorite practice to take with you on your continuing journey to inner peace.

YOUR INNER CIRCLE OF SUPPORT
WEEK 3, DAY 2

To fulfill your essential need for belonging, you need a circle of support, a community of trust to nurture and sustain you.

Your innermost circle includes your romantic partner and your "psychological family" who love and support you whether you're biologically related or not (P. Boss, personal communication, November 10, 2023). My inner circle includes close friendships with women who've become like sisters, sharing our hopes, dreams, and personal challenges. Research has shown how profoundly such relationships can promote our emotional and physical health (Mikulincer et al., 2005).

Your inner circle is based on *quality* connections (Dutton & Heaphy, 2003). Having thousands of "friends" on social media is no substitute for personal relationships that offer deep connection, mutual love, and support. These are positive relationships, based not on "shoulds" and obligations. They're not transactional, based on how much one person can get from another, or codependent, where we keep striving to "earn" approval. Empowering and energizing, these positive relationships contrast with depleting relationships that can leave us feeling drained and exhausted.

In your inner circle, you are seen and valued, experiencing the trust, understanding, and comfort that sustain you, especially when you're feeling challenged (Dutton & Heaphy, 2003). Connecting you in a bond of mutual love and respect that philosopher Martin Buber (1956) described as "I-Thou," these relationships have a rhythm of giving and receiving, a process as natural as breathing in and breathing out. Because I grew up in a dysfunctional family, it took me quite a while to realize that I didn't need to do all the giving, that I could ask my friends for help. In fact, research (Snyder, 1994) has found that asking for help when we need it is not a sign of weakness but a vital skill that strengthens our hope.

Many people develop close friendships when they face mutual challenges in their education, careers, or military service. I met my friend Pat Patrick in graduate school at UCLA. Pat was an aspiring novelist, who lived in Hollywood and knew actors, rock musicians, and screen writers. I lived in Santa Monica, inspired by yoga, meditation, and the Pacific Ocean. But beyond our differences, we developed a strong bond of connection, sharing our challenges, discoveries, and aspirations after class, over coffee, or in late night phone calls. Giving and receiving, we learned a lot from each other.

Years later, our differences have increased while our connection has only grown stronger. I became a college professor, teaching Renaissance literature and creative writing. Pat took a day job in San Francisco, focusing on her writing. When she married Gary, they moved to a cabin in the redwoods. Dedicated to protecting the land, they lived close to nature like Thoreau and Pat continued to write.

We still share our hopes and fears, challenges, and dreams. I live in California's Silicon Valley, writing on a laptop, participating in podcasts, webinars, and Zoom conferences. After Gary's passing, Pat still lives off the grid in her cabin near the Oregon border, writing on a manual typewriter, and chopping firewood for her stove. We write long handwritten letters like people did centuries ago. She tells of stocking up for winter, when mudslides block the winding mountain roads. We share stories of our gardens, including the ripe tomatoes we enjoy each summer. We discuss books—last year we read *War and Peace* together. And we discuss our meditative practices, offering consolation, inspiration, and support. Giving and receiving. When I see a letter from Pat in my mailbox, I'm filled with gratitude for our spiritual sisterhood that brings greater light to my life.

Exercise: Your Inner Circle of Support.

Now it's your turn. Can you recall a time you felt loved and supported by a close friend or family member? Because these relationships thrive with the rhythm of giving and receiving, think of one way you can cultivate a deeper sense of connection with this person or with someone else you care about.

Write down your experience and your action plan here or in your journal.

****

Inner Circle of Support Practice: _____

Date

I've felt a loving sense of connection with

_____

When we were

_____

This week I will reach out to cultivate a deeper sense of connection with [who]

_____

By doing [what] _____

YOUR EXPANDING CIRCLE
WEEK 3, Day 3

Like the planets in our solar system, we are not alone in the universe but surrounded by the light of concentric circles of relationship.

We need to consciously connect to this expansive circle of community. Research has found that the amount of social connection in our lives is one of the most consistent predictors of health and wellbeing (Collins et al., 2022).

Feeling separate and isolated is not only unnatural, but unhealthy. Studies have shown that when people focus excessively on themselves, constantly using the pronouns "I," "me," "my," and "mine," they're at greater risk for depression and cardiovascular disease (Zimmerman et al., 2017; Schwerwitz et al., 1986). Apparently, our hearts *need* connection with others.

We also need "relational diversity" (Collins et al., 2022), widening circles of connection, not only at home, but at work and in our local communities.

I enjoy walking around the neighborhood with my little dog Ginny, waving to neighbors driving by or talking to people we meet along the way. As research (Fredrickson, 2013) has shown, even short, casual interactions like these can bring us major benefits, relieving stress and promoting greater physical and emotional well-being for both people involved. And over time, these small acts of connection can help build more connected communities.

We can also build community when we come together for a common purpose in our jobs or volunteer work. When I became chair of Santa Clara University's English department, my efforts to build community involved everything from improved communication and collective decision making to bringing food to the department office. At the beginning of each academic year, I'd bring bagels, lox, cream cheese, and fresh fruit to our department mail room for a "new year's brunch," and throughout the year I'd provide an occasional surprise of homemade cookies or cakes. Our mail room became a gathering place where we'd share campus news, jokes, and a sense of community.

Drawing on our collective wisdom, I began a new tradition of voting on department policies and budget priorities. I'd keep my office door open for my colleagues to drop by with questions and concerns, and I wrote a weekly memo, listing campus deadlines and meetings, along with our recent accomplishments. Our department became a community where we laughed and learned together, our teaching and scholarship flourished, and hundreds of students chose to major in English.

We can all take small steps to cultivate community. You can cultivate your local community by shopping at nearby stores instead of ordering so many things online. To stay safer during the COVID pandemic, many of us had supplies and groceries delivered. But if we continue to substitute convenience for community, our local shops will close, communities will erode, and we will all become more isolated.

My town's Ace Hardware store has become a local community center where neighbors greet each other, high school students work their first jobs, and older adults offer friendly advice and mentoring. I enjoy going there for garden supplies, tools, and helpful advice on my many projects.

A few years ago, developers were planning to buy the property and cancel Ace Hardware's lease in order to build a high-rise office building. But when the developers presented their proposal to the town council, I joined my neighbors in the council chamber—parents and children, high school students, working professionals, and retired people. One by one, we stood at the podium, sharing our stories of how Ace Hardware was a vital part of our community. When the council members rejected the developers' proposal, we left the meeting celebrating that together we'd preserved this vital place of connection and community.

In these uncertain times, we can also cultivate community by listening and learning from each other, especially people with different views from ours. Research has found that many people are threatened by differences and uncertainty (MacDonald, 1970). But according to *New York Times* columnist David Brooks (2023), listening, learning, and connecting more deeply with each other can help heal the painful polarization, misunderstanding, and hostility in our world.

When we meet someone new, we can become more mindfully present, listen actively, ask questions, reflect on what we've heard, and search for common ground. For there is always common ground. It's the world of connection we share on this beautiful planet we call home.

Exercise: Your Expanding Circle.

Now it's your turn. Can you recall a time you felt part of an expanding circle of connection at work or school, in your neighborhood or in one of your other communities? Then think of one step you can take to cultivate greater connection with your expanding circle. Can you do something in your neighborhood? At work? In your town? Or reach out to communicate with people who hold different views?

Write your experience and one way you'll connect here or in your journal.

****

Your Expanding Circle Practice: _____

                                                   Date

I've felt an expansive sense of connection with

_____

When I was _____

This week I will reach out to connect with my expanding circle by

_____

SPIRITUAL COMPANIONSHIP
WEEK 3, Day 4

Some relationships can take us beyond ourselves, connecting us to an enduring source of joy and inspiration. This can happen with a loved one, a dear friend, or a spiritual community. Romantic love can inspire us, as poets have written for centuries. Dante's love for Beatrice led him to a vision of "the love that moves the sun and the other stars" (1921, line 145).

Sometimes, we can find spiritual companionship with a dear friend as I did with Brad Parker when I was in college. The year before we met, I'd been a senior at a military high school in Germany, filling out my college applications and dreaming of going to UCLA. That summer, visions of college life filled my head as my family moved to my father's new assignment at Norton Air Force Base in southern California. In August, I was packing up for UCLA when my mother came into my bedroom and announced, "Your father and I have transferred your acceptance to the University of California, Riverside so you don't have to go away to college. You can ride to school with Colonel Parker's son across the street."

"Why?" I asked, feeling shocked and betrayed. "We can't afford it," she said and left the room. Their finances were not really the issue; my mother got a new Mercedes that year for Christmas, but that's another story. So, when classes began, I rode out to the Riverside campus with Colonel Parker's son.

Brad Parker's parents were divorced, and he'd just arrived from New York City where he'd been living with his mother. In my mind, New York was a magical place—the land of the Roosevelts, book publishers, Broadway shows, the New York Philharmonic, and the Statue of Liberty.

Fascinated, I asked Brad about life in New York, then learned we had a lot in common. We were both spiritual seekers, eager to explore new worlds of ideas. "What's on your mind?" he'd ask with a smile. He'd lend me books on Eastern philosophy, and I began meditating.

Brad encouraged me to look beneath the surface, to seek the deeper meaning of life, and believe in my dreams. His enthusiasm was empowering. "Fantastic!" was his favorite word. We'd converse in the car and spend hours talking, laughing, and drinking coffee in his room across the street, discussing meditation, our spiritual journeys, personal challenges, and goals. His stepmother would peer in the door and eavesdrop, wondering what on earth we were doing, so we'd shift into French, which I'd studied in high school and Brad had learned in Belgium when he'd lived there with his Air Force father.

Two years later, we both moved beyond the suburban world of our parents. Brad worked all summer, saved his money, and transferred to the University of California, Santa Barbara. I got a part-time job, moved into the Riverside college dorms, worked my way through college, and then went on to graduate school at UCLA. Although our paths took different directions, I'll always be grateful to Brad for sharing his dynamic New York attitude and opening my eyes to my spiritual journey.

Many people throughout time have found inspiration in spiritual friendships. Ralph Waldo Emerson and Henry David Thoreau shared a deep friendship and love of nature. Spiritual companionship can transcend cultural differences. Christian pastor and civil rights leader Martin Luther King shared a spiritual friendship with Buddhist teacher Thich Nhat Hanh, and the Dalai Lama found such a friendship with Archbishop Desmond Tutu.

Our spiritual companions can continue to inspire us, even beyond time. Psychologist Dacher Keltner, PhD, does research on awe, the expansive wonder we can experience in nature, art, and connection with those we love. He grew up sharing a deep spiritual bond with his brother Rolf, hiking together in the mountains. After his brother's passing, when Dacher is out in nature, he still senses Rolf's presence in the gentle breezes and the warm embrace of the sun (Keltner, 2023).

Some of us find spiritual companionship in traditional religions. Research has shown that participating in a church, temple, or mosque can bring us a sense of belonging and coherence (Antonovsky, 1980). Connecting us to something greater than ourselves, religious participation has been linked to better emotional and physical health (George et al., 2002).

Many people participate in less formal spiritual communities, coming together to meditate and share their values, beliefs, and personal challenges. A term for this kind of community is Satsang, from the Sanskrit "*Sat*," (truth) and "*Sang*," (together), literally "people who seek truth together." I find inspiration in a local group that meets monthly to meditate at a nearby lake and in a local weekly Satsang group.

Berkeley sociology professor Susan Phillips cultivates Satsang as a spiritual director, taking small groups of people through the Ignatian Spiritual Exercises, developed by the Catholic Saint Ignatius Loyola. They meet for two-hour weekly sessions, meditating on Biblical passages and sharing insights, questions, and concerns. Before COVID, the groups met in person, but since then they've met virtually. Phillips has found that the Spiritual Exercises offer people from many denominations an experience of spiritual connection, comfort, and community (2022).

As a sociologist, Susan Phillips realizes how much we need group support. She's concerned that much of our culture "has lost a lot of that communal intimacy" (personal communication, December 11, 2023).

In an effort to build such vital support, Andre Delbecq, former dean of Santa Clara University's Business School, began a series of "Spirituality for CEOs" seminars, bringing together busy Silicon Valley executives to share their hopes, values, and leadership challenges.

Andre Delbecq (2010) also founded a spiritual community for Santa Clara University faculty in which I've served as facilitator. Twelve faculty members and two facilitators meet one day a month for four-hour meetings that begin at 4pm when we check in and discuss readings from spiritual and psychological texts. We then share a simple soup supper before a final session when we bring our personal and professional challenges to the group for shared discernment and support. Over the years, I've seen how groups of faculty members with diverse beliefs—Catholic, Protestant, Jewish, Islamic, and agnostic— see beyond our differences to recognize our common purpose, becoming communities of trust and mutual support.

We are all on journeys, seeking more heart-centered, peaceful, and meaningful lives. Finding companions on the journey can bring us greater understanding and stronger connection to our deepest values, one another, and our world.

Exercise: Spiritual Community.

Now it's your turn. Can you recall a time you felt deep spiritual companionship with a loved one, a dear friend, or spiritual community? Or if you haven't experienced it yet, what might spiritual companionship look like for you?

Think of one step you can take to cultivate spiritual companionship in your life this week, which might involve getting in touch with a dear friend, participating in a spiritual community, or something else.

Write your experience and one way you'll connect here or in your journal.

****

Spiritual Companionship Practice: _____

                                                            Date

I've felt spiritual companionship with _____

or

This is how I might envision spiritual companionship in my own life

_____

This week I will reach out to begin cultivating or deepening spiritual companionship by

_____

ANIMAL COMPANIONS
WEEK 3, DAY 5

Many of us have felt a sense of connection and comfort with a beloved animal companion.

When I was five years old, my family had a black Labrador retriever named Cinder, and I loved her dearly. We lived in Louisville, Kentucky where my father was a pilot, often gone on long flights. My mother was preoccupied with my baby brother and her own activities, so Cinder would watch over me. Every morning, my dog would walk me down the street to kindergarten, then walk back to the house. Every afternoon at 3:00—Cinder could apparently tell time—she'd walk back to school to bring me home.

Cinder was my loving companion, my guardian, and my best friend. But then my father was transferred to Washington, D.C. We had to move, and my parents gave Cinder away to a farmer outside Louisville. A few days later, when we were moving into our new house in Maryland, my parents got a phone call from our former neighbor in Kentucky. Cinder had walked for miles from the farm back to our old house in Louisville, and was sitting on the front steps waiting for us. But my parents left her in Kentucky. I still feel sad when I remember.

Today, people are more aware of the bond of loving compassion between people and their dogs. We now know that dogs often serve as attachment figures for children, fostering loving security, trust, and confidence (Maharaj et al., 2014).

Research has revealed that dogs can have a calming effect on their owners, helping to console them when they are upset and bring them back to the present moment (Maharaj et al., 2016). When I'm caught up in worry, compulsive planning, and multitasking, my little dog Ginny brings me back to a sense of presence and connection.

Studies have linked pet ownership with lower blood pressure, increased exercise, and stronger immunity (Nimer & Lundahl, 2007). Our animal companions can also be good for our emotional health. Research at the University of Liverpool in England has found that pets can provide unconditional love and affection, reduce worry and rumination, and promote greater self-acceptance. People in the Liverpool study said that their pets relieved their anxiety and depression, providing a sense of trust and purpose. One woman said she could talk to her cat when she couldn't confide in other people, and a young girl said that when she began crying, her dog would come and lick her face to comfort her (H. L. Brooks et al. 2018).

Research has shown that animal companionship can be profoundly therapeutic. Service dogs can recognize the signs of Post Traumatic Stress Disorder in veterans and soothe them when they get anxious and distressed (Yount et al., 2013). Therapy dogs in hospitals can help children recover by reducing anxiety, stress, and loneliness. Relating to the dogs brings them joy, decreases their need for medication, and even improves their physical function (Fontaine et al,, 2001). Animal-assisted therapy with dogs, cats, horses, dolphins, rabbits, and birds has helped people with physical, emotional, neurological, and psychiatric issues, and a friendly dog in a psychotherapist's office can often enhance the therapy, providing acceptance and promoting greater trust, comfort, and calm (Netting et al., 1987; Nimer & Lundahl, 2007; Silcox, et al., 2014).

Our animal companions can help relieve loneliness, which is so pervasive in our world today. Social workers have found that a loving bond with a dog or cat can comfort lonely people, improving their health, and restoring their hope (Netting, et al., 1987).

There are many ways we can experience animal companionship. Some of my friends have dogs and cats. Other friends have horses, birds, fish tanks, or koi ponds. One friend volunteers at a local animal shelter. Others simply enjoy pausing and talking to neighbors who are walking their dogs. Some people I know are avid bird watchers. I relate to my wild animal neighbors by setting hummingbird and bird seed feeders outside my window and leaving nuts for squirrels in a tree in my back yard.

Exercise: Animal Companions.

What is one step you could take this week to cultivate greater companionship with the animals in your world? If you have a dog or cat, how can you relate to them more mindfully? Or can you connect more with your wild animal neighbors?

Write your experience and one way you'll connect here or in your journal.

****

Animal Companion Practice: _____

Date

I enjoy animal companionship with

_____

One way I'll cultivate greater animal companionship this week is by

_____

YOUR SENSE OF HOME
WEEK 3, DAY 6

To feel connected to our world, we all need a sense of home. According to Canadian educator Kim Samuel (2022, p. 101), "Our sense of home is essential to an experience of belonging." Research has described home as a refuge, a place where we feel safe and secure, where we find acceptance, comfort, and renewal (Després, 1991; Mallett, 2004).

For many of us, "home" is where we grew up. But for years, when people asked me, "Where are you from?" I didn't know what to say. I'd moved across the country and around the world with my Air Force father on his many assignments. By the time I graduated from Kaiserslautern American High School in Germany, I'd attended ten different schools. All that moving made me more flexible and more aware of different cultures and ways of life. But I also felt something was missing from my life. Research has shown that children of military families who move frequently can feel a sense of rootlessness, anxiety, and insecurity (Morris et al., 2017; S. Taylor, 2022).

In my twenties, I developed a strong connection to UCLA. My five years there in graduate school were the longest time I'd ever lived anywhere. Then, I moved to northern California to teach at Santa Clara University. A few years later, on a flight back from a conference, I looked out the airplane window at the beautiful valley below and realized I was coming home. The San Francisco Bay area has been my home ever since.

As the Renaissance poet John Donne wrote, "No man is an island" (1624/1965, p. 108). We are part of something larger than ourselves, and we can find our sense of home by connecting on multiple levels. Czech playwright and political leader Vaclav Havel (1992) described home as a multidimensional experience in which we're surrounded by concentric circles of connection from our families and close friends to our neighborhoods, towns, workplaces, countries, and the world in which we live.

I resonate with Havel's vision, feeling comfort, connection, and a sense of home with my family, friends, neighborhood, community, country, and world. I'm grateful to have shared my life with a dear partner who brought me a deep and loving sense of home. For years, I've felt a sense of home at my university, in my neighborhood and the town where I live. I enjoy joining with others to work for causes I believe in, and I find companionship and comfort in my garden. Grateful for the green cathedral of trees surrounding my yard, I realize how intimately we're connected as I breathe in what the trees breathe out.

I love interacting with nature's annual cycle of growth where there is always something happening if we only look closely enough—glorious red and gold autumn leaves, the dark, quiet season of winter, new growth pushing up through the soil in early spring, flowers blooming, and vegetables to harvest from summer to fall.

But many of us have lost our sense of home. Years ago, I counseled homeless women at a San Jose shelter. These women were literally homeless. Most had lost their homes because of job layoffs and financial emergencies. But as Kim Samuel (2022) has explained, many of us are *virtually* homeless. We've lost our sense of belonging, the deep relationships we need with the people, places, and natural world around us.

Many of our circles of connection were lost in the COVID pandemic. In my community, our local drugstore closed, along with my favorite bookstore and the coffee shop where I'd meet my friend Tina for lunch.

Our sense of home is also eroding because of changing corporate and government practices. Nearly every week I hear of tech companies laying off hundreds of employees. And our federal government has been slashing jobs in many agencies. Deprived of their salaries and workplace connections, many people's lives are being disrupted. They're forced to seek new jobs, and many of them will move away from their communities.

But there are also people who recognize the importance of community. In 1995, after a devastating fire at his factory, Aaron Feuerstein, the CEO of Malden Mills in Lawrence, Massachusetts, made the national news by continuing to pay his employees' salaries and benefits for months while rebuilding the factory.

Exercise: Your Sense of Home.

Your efforts may not be as dramatic as Aaron Feuerstein's, but you, too, can build a stronger sense of home for yourself and our world.

- *You can begin by pausing to mindfully appreciate the beauty in your own living space, neighborhood, and community. Taking small steps, you can cultivate a greater sense of refuge and comfort where you live, perhaps by hanging a favorite picture on the wall, putting a comfortable chair by the window, or curling up with a warm blanket.*

- *You can also clear away items you no longer need and share them with your community. I enjoy sharing books with my neighbors by donating them to the Little Free Library down the street.*

- *You can cultivate a stronger sense of home in your community by greeting your neighbors, colleagues, and the people you see each day.*

- *You can volunteer for causes you believe in, taking action to protect your community and our natural environment.*

- *And at the end of the day, you can look up at the sky to connect with the universe of stars sparkling overhead.*

Can you think of a time you've felt a deep sense of home? Then think of one step you could take this week to cultivate a greater sense of home within and around you.

Write your experience and one way you'll connect with a sense of home here or in your journal.

****

Your Sense of Home Practice: _____

                               Date

I've felt a deep sense of home when

_____

One way I'll cultivate a stronger sense of home in my life is by

_____

RELECT AND REVIEW
WEEK 3, DAY 7

This week, you were invited to try these practices:

1. Your Circle of Support

2. Your Expanding Circle

3. Spiritual Companionship

4. Animal Companions

5. Your Sense of Home

As you look back on your week, reflect on your responses. Review how each practice made you feel, and choose at least one practice you'd like to take along on your journey to greater peace of mind. Write down your experience here or in your journal.

****

Week 3 Review: _____

                        Date

What practice would you like to take with you?

_____

What feelings does this practice inspire for you?

_____

How can you use this practice to develop greater peace of mind in the days to come?

_____

CHAPTER 4

The Path of Meditation

PREPARATION
WEEK 4: DAY 1

Meditation can bring us a sense of peace and connection with the oneness of life.

I began meditating years ago and now begin my days with a brief moment of mindfulness. As I open my bedroom window and look out at the world each morning, I see the sunlight shining through the trees, the blue sky and clouds drifting overhead, the dynamic, living landscape that surrounds me. Pausing to take a few deep mindful breaths at the beginning of the day keeps my mind from racing ahead with anxious planning as I focus my attention on the gift of this day, this present moment.

Moments of mindfulness can bring us back to our essential connection with life. Trauma specialist Gabor Maté, MD, (2022) has found that meditation can help us heal from the traumatizing effects of a culture that often makes us feel that we are not safe. Far too often, our contemporary culture can fragment our attention, undermine our peace of mind, and even compromise our health (McEwen & Lasley, 2002; Osborne et al, 2020).

Meditation can heal us physically and promote greater wellbeing by relieving our anxiety, lowering our blood pressure, reducing inflammation, and strengthening our immune systems (Garland, 2007; Hoge et al, 2023; Jacobs et al, 2011; Jevning et al., 1988; Rosenkranz et al., 2016).

Meditation can also heal us emotionally by reducing feelings of loneliness and isolation, connecting us to a greater sense of oneness with nature, one another, and a deeper sense of ourselves (Creswell et al., 2012; Wahbeh et al., 2018).

Many years ago, while meditating at his cabin at Walden Pond, Henry David Thoreau experienced this deep sense of oneness with nature. "I love a broad margin to my life" he wrote. "Sometimes, in a summer morning, . . . I sat in my sunny doorway from sunrise till noon. . .in undisturbed solitude and stillness, while the birds sang around or flitted noiselessly through the house, . . .I grew in those seasons like corn in the night" (1960, p. 89). As Thoreau realized, meditation can help us grow emotionally and spiritually, opening us up to a deep source of inspiration.

Meditation has long been part of many spiritual traditions. As psychologist William James recognized, it's been practiced around the world for centuries in Christianity, Judaism, Buddhism, Hinduism, Taoism, Islam, and Native American religions (1902/1985).

Neuroscience research has shown how meditation can bring us a sense of comfort, connection, and inner peace by quieting the constant chatter of our minds (L. Miller et al, 2018; Newberg et al., 2001; Sheldrake, 2017). Deeper levels of meditation can fill us with joy, enabling us to transcend the boundaries between our separate selves and the larger world (Wahbeh et al., 2018).

Research has shown that meditation can help us create greater harmony within and around us by making us kinder, more compassionate, and more altruistic (Vieten et al., 2006). In an affirmation of hope for our time, Larry Dossey, MD, (2013) says that experiencing the sense of oneness in meditation can help us overcome the disconnection, divisiveness, selfishness, and violence threatening our lives and our world.

Even if you haven't practiced meditation before, you may have felt the sense of transcendent oneness known as awe when you experienced the beauty of nature or a magnificent work of art (Keltner, 2023). In such times, as Ralph

Waldo Emerson would say, our separate "egotism vanishes" as we feel a deep sense of connection to all that is (1903, p. 10).

A few years ago, when I heard Jon Kabat-Zinn, Ph.D., give a talk at Santa Clara University, a woman in the audience stood up and asked how he could spend so much time meditating when there are so many urgent problems in the world. Jon paused, smiled, and said that at Boston Symphony Orchestra concerts, he's noticed how the musicians always tune their instruments before they begin performing. Meditation, he said, is how we tune our instruments.

In this chapter, you will discover how you can tune your own instrument with meditation practices that can help you see more clearly, act more wisely, and bring greater harmony to our world.

Exercise: Setting Your Intention

Now it's time to set your intention for the week. (For example, "My intention is to find greater connection in meditation.")

It's important to write down this intention as an invitation to yourself. You can record it here or in your journal.

My intention is _____

Today's Date

Now take a moment to connect with your intention.

- *Take a deep breath and slowly release it.*
- *Recall a time in your life when you felt a deep sense of comfort and connection.*
- *Where were you and what were you doing?*

Remember this feeling to maintain your intention as you practice the meditation exercises in the days ahead.

Each day this week, you'll find a new meditation practice. Try these practices one day at a time, and if one practice doesn't appeal to you, just repeat another practice. At the end of the week, as you look back and reflect on your experience, choose a favorite meditation practice to take with you on your continuing journey to inner peace.

MINDFULNESS MEDITATION
WEEK 4, DAY 2

"What is more easy and sweet than meditation?" wrote Renaissance poet Thomas Traherne (1908/1960, p. 5). Centuries ago, he saw meditation as a way to heal our fragmented lives and bring us greater wholeness and harmony—a timely practice for us all in our challenging world today.

We'll begin our meditative practices this week with a simple version of mindfulness meditation. This form of meditation opens us up to our essential interconnectedness. For we are already connected—to our minds, our feelings, and our bodies, to one another and our world. What mindfulness meditation does is make us *aware* of this connection.

If you've never meditated before, you may have thought meditation required uncomfortable postures and rigorous concentration. But as experienced meditation teachers explain, mindfulness meditation can be easier than all that, involving simple awareness and resting in the present moment (Mingyur Rinpoche, 2007).

Mindfulness meditation is a process of relaxing and observing the natural state of your awareness. It does *not* mean stopping your thoughts. Instead, it involves observing them without attachment, letting your thoughts, feelings, and sensations flow by in the inner stream of your awareness.

Exercise: Mindfulness Meditation

To begin mindfulness meditation, find a time and place where you won't be disturbed. Sit comfortably in a chair or even on the floor, with your back straight and your body relaxed, for a brief 5-10 -minute session. If you wish, you can set a timer before you start.

Then with your eyes closed or gently gazing down, begin focusing on your breathing.

- *Take a slow, deep mindful breath, feeling the breath flow through your body.*

- *Then continue to focus on your breathing as you gradually breathe out, releasing any tension with each outbreath.*

- *Breathing in.*

- *Breathing out.*

- *When you find yourself becoming distracted by a thought, feeling, or noise around you—and you will—simply note the distraction, silently saying to yourself, "thinking," "feeling," or "hearing." Then gently return your awareness to your breathing.*

- *These distractions and returns don't mean you're failing at meditation. They are an essential part of the process. Like the "reps" lifting weights at the gym, repeating this process over time can make you stronger.*

If you'd like to continue the practice after this week, you might want to stay with this brief meditation period or gradually extend the time to 20-30 minutes once or twice a day. I begin my days with meditation to tune my instrument as Jon Kabat-Zinn describes it. Then I meditate again in the evening to release all the busyness of the day.

Practice a brief 5-10-minute mindfulness meditation once today. Then record your experience here or in your journal.

****

Mindfulness Meditation Practice:_____

                                                              Date

When did you do it? _____

What was your experience? _____

HEART COHERENCE MEDITATION
WEEK 4, DAY 3

Research at the HeartMath Institute in Northern California has found that meditation promotes greater peace of mind by creating coherence—more harmonious heart rhythms and greater balance in our nervous systems. The institute has developed various forms of heart coherence meditation, which can reduce stress, improve mental clarity, and lead to better health (Childre et al., 2016). Research has even shown that people who practiced heart coherence meditation daily for four weeks experienced positive changes in their brains (Min et al., 2023).

Demonstrating how we are all interconnected, HeartMath researchers have found that when we achieve greater heart coherence, our harmonious energies can also promote greater peace of mind in those around us. Their studies have shown how one person's heart coherence can positively affect other people in the same room. They've also found that our coherent energies can also positively affect our pets and create a bond of connection that helps teams perform more harmoniously (Childre et al., 2016).

I've done heart coherence meditation for years now and noticed how much more relaxed I feel. I've even noticed my dog becoming more relaxed during my meditations.

Exercise: Heart Coherence Meditation

HeartMath coherence techniques combine mindful breathing with an added focus on the heart (Childre et al., p. 82). Here is a quick version you can practice today.

The Quick Coherence® Technique

Step 1. Focus your attention in the area of the heart. Imagine your breath is flowing in and out of your heart or chest area, breathing a little slower and deeper than usual. Find an easy rhythm that is comfortable.

Step 2. As you continue heart-focused breathing, make a sincere attempt to experience a regenerative feeling such as appreciation or care for someone or something in your life.

The Quick Coherence® Technique was developed by HeartMath and is a registered trademark of HeartMath. HeartMath is a registered trademark of Quantum Intech, Inc. For all HeartMath trademarks, go to www.heartmath.com/trademarks.

You can practice Quick Coherence for ten minutes or more as a regular meditation practice. And when you're feeling stressed, you can also use a short version for a minute or two to gain greater peace of mind.

Practice Quick Coherence once today. At the end of the day, record your experience here or in your journal.

****

Quick Coherence Practice:_____

                                                            Date

When did you do it? _____

What was your experience? _____

CENTERING PRAYER MEDITATION
WEEK 4, DAY 4

Years ago, I spent many happy afternoons in centering prayer meditation with Jane Ferguson at St. Mary's Church in my town. As the stained-glass windows glowed with the light of the afternoon sun, a small group of us used to sit in a circle by the altar in comforting silence while we practiced our centering meditation. This form of meditation dates back to the early desert fathers and was re-introduced in our time by Fr. Thomas Keating.

While serving as Director of Pastoral Care at St. Mary's, Jane wrote her doctoral dissertation on the benefits of centering prayer. She discovered that this practice not only relieves stress and promotes relaxation but can even help heal emotional wounds by bringing deep inner peace to the unconscious (Ferguson, 2010). Jane has found that centering prayer can enable us to "rest in God in the midst of intense daily struggle" (Ferguson, 2010, p. 63) as we deal with the multiple challenges in our lives today.

Centering prayer is similar to mindfulness meditation but adds a sacred word to quiet the mind. You can adapt this form of meditation to your own needs and preferences, beginning with this ten-minute practice.

Exercise: Centering Prayer Meditation

- *First choose a sacred word for your meditation. Traditional centering prayer uses words like "Jesus," or "Shalom." You can choose a word from your own tradition or another word meaningful to you such as "peace" "joy," "om," or "love."*

- *Then sitting comfortably with your eyes closed, silently say the sacred word to yourself to open up to greater peace within.*

- *When your mind wanders, say the sacred word silently to yourself to return to the stillness.*

- *At the end of the practice, remain still with your eyes closed for a final moment (Ferguson, 2010).*

Then, open your eyes and return to your daily activities.

If you'd like to continue Centering Prayer after this week, you can practice it daily. Jane recommends gradually extending your meditation time to 20 minutes.

When you've practiced Centering Prayer today, record your experience here or in your journal

****

Centering Prayer Meditation Practice: _____

                                                   Date

When did you do it? _____

What was your experience? _____

PASSAGE MEDITATION
WEEK 4, DAY 5

For years, I've practiced passage meditation each day. Years ago, I even meditated on my favorite passage while getting a root canal, surprising the endodontist by being so relaxed and peaceful. I've found passage meditation especially comforting lately when dealing with personal loss, challenges, change, and uncertainty.

Passage meditation can help us deal with involuntary negative thoughts circling through our minds that drain and diminish us, thoughts like "You're not good enough, smart enough, attractive enough, or successful enough." My husband Bob, a neuroscientist, once told me that we all have a "negativity bias" that automatically makes us focus on threats to our survival (Rozin, & Royzman, 2001). This bias keeps us vigilant, on guard, and judgmental, especially of ourselves. While it may keep us safe in dangerous situations, most of the time the negativity bias can make us feel inadequate and insecure.

Passage meditation can replace this succession of negative thoughts with slow, focused attention on inspirational passages from the world's spiritual traditions.

In the past few years, many of us have experienced an underlying anxiety, insecurity, and lack of trust in our world. Meditation teacher Eknath Easwaran (2016, p. 11) taught that passage meditation can connect us to abiding truths that "put a final end to insecurity." As we meditate, the inspiring words can fill our minds with a deeper reality, bringing greater light to our lives.

You can practice passage meditation by choosing an inspirational passage or poem from your own tradition.

Or you can follow the example of Easwaran, who discovered after years of teaching meditation, that the prayer of St. Francis of Assisi has "almost universal appeal" (2016, p. 1). While not written by St. Francis himself, it incorporates many themes from his spiritual teachings. I've found that this passage helps me move beyond my isolated, disconnected self to a sense of loving connection to all that is.

The Prayer of St. Francis

Lord, make me an instrument of thy peace.

Where there is hatred, let me sow love;

Where there is injury, pardon;

Where there is doubt, faith;

Where there is despair, hope;

Where there is darkness, light;

Where there is sadness, joy.

O divine Master, grant that I may not so much seek

To be consoled as to console,

To be understood as to understand,

To be loved as to love;

For it is in giving that we receive;

It is in pardoning that we are pardoned;

It is in dying to self that we are born to eternal life (Easwaran, 2016, pp. 1-2).

Exercise: Passage Meditation

You can begin passage meditation with an inspirational passage of your choice. If you've memorized it, you can close your eyes, then slowly and silently focus on the passage.

Or you can begin meditating on a passage by reading one line, then closing your eyes and silently repeating it to yourself, repeating this process as you slowly go through the passage one line at a time.

As you're meditating, when your mind wanders, gently bring your full attention back to the passage.

Practice passage meditation for ten minutes once today. If you'd like to continue this meditation after this week, you can practice it daily. Easwaran (2016) recommends gradually extending your meditation time to 30 minutes and meditating first thing in the morning. You may want to experiment with what works best for you.

After you've practiced passage meditation, record your experience here or in your journal.

****

Passage Meditation Practice: _____

Date

When did you do it?

_____

What was your experience? _____

MOVING MEDITATION
WEEK 4, DAY 6

Spiritual traditions throughout the ages have combined meditation with movement. When I taught yoga at the East-West Center for the Healing Arts, our practice combined physical postures with meditation and open-hearted oneness. In fact, the word *yoga* means "union," helping us overcome the sense of separation by uniting mind, heart, and body (Easwaran, 2001, p. 59).

In addition to yoga, forms of moving meditation include *chi gong* and *tai chi* from China and *aikido* from Japan. These practices can help us focus and extend our vital energies (*chi* in Chinese, *ki* in Japanese). For years, I trained in aikido, a nonviolent martial art that enables us to focus, extend our *ki,* and transform conflict without harming our opponent, a practice I found centering, exhilarating, and empowering.

All moving meditation involves being present to the process of our movement as we connect with the vital energies within and around us. You may already have a moving meditation that works for you. My husband Bob found his in running, feeling one with the wind. My friend Tracey would go for meditative walks in the redwoods.

Research has shown that walking in a natural setting can relieve depression and anxiety (Berman et al., 2012; F.S. Mayer et al., 2009). I witnessed this transformative effect for myself a few years ago when counseling homeless women at a San Jose shelter.

When I first met Louise, she was slumped down in her chair, her eyes downcast, feeling ashamed and hopeless. A deeply religious African American woman, she had worked all her life, sending money back to her family in Mississippi. Then suddenly her company downsized, laying her off, and her landlord sold her apartment building to a developer who evicted all the tenants. Louise moved into a motel and applied for jobs until her car broke down and her savings ran out.

Now here she was, downcast, isolated, and alone. She couldn't even get to church without a car. But we came up with a plan. Louise would walk each day in a nearby park, combining walking with passage meditation, reciting her favorite 23rd psalm.

When I met with her a week later, I was amazed by her transformation. Smiling and professionally dressed, she'd already applied for low-income housing and set up several job interviews. By walking in the park, looking up at the trees and sky, and saying her inspirational passage to herself, Louise realized that she was not alone and discovered renewed hope.

Exercise: Moving Meditation

To practice moving meditation today, if you already have a favorite practice like yoga, tai chi, or running, you can spend some time practicing it. If not, then you could take a short meditative nature walk in your yard or a nearby park.

If you'd like to take a nature walk, here's one way you can practice moving meditation:

- *Slow down, focus on your breathing, and mindfully connect with the green world around you. Look at the patterns in the trees and sky.*

- *Hear the wind rustling through the leaves. Feel the gentle breeze or the warm sun on your skin.*

- *Then look for a message of hope—bright green leaves on a tree or shrub, a wildflower growing through a crack in the sidewalk, a bird singing in the trees overhead, or something else.*

- *What does this message mean to you—Comfort? Harmony? Perseverance? Something you need to learn?*

- *Remember the message as you come back from your walk and return to your regular activities.*

Practice your moving meditation for at least ten minutes today. Then record your experience here or in your journal.

****

Moving Meditation Practice: _____

                                    Date

When did you do it? _____

What was your experience? _____

WEEK 4, DAY 7: Reflect and Review

This week, you were invited to try these meditative practices:

1. Mindfulness Meditation

2. Heart Coherence Meditation

3. Centering Prayer Meditation

4. Passage Meditation

5. Moving Meditation

As you look back on your week, reflect on your responses. Review how each practice made you feel, and choose at least one practice you'd like to take along on your journey to greater peace of mind. Then, record your experience here or in your journal.

****

Week 4 Review: _____

Date

What practice would you like to take with you?

_____

What feelings does this practice inspire for you?

_____

How can you use this practice to develop greater peace of mind in the days to come?

_____

CHAPTER 5

The Path of Kindness

PREPARATION
WEEK 5, DAY 1

My friend Genevieve Farrow once gave me a picture with smiling angel faces surrounding the words, "All commandments can be reduced to one: loving kindness." This picture has been hanging on my wall for years, but its message is now even more timely. For lately, many of us have been living with a constant stream of worries and fears filling our minds, telling us that we are not safe.

If we've been living in fear, it's because we see our world as divided and disconnected. Yet, as the picture reminds me, we can find peace, renewal, and transformation with the power of loving kindness.

As psychologist Steve Taylor (2022) explains, Western culture's emphasis on individualism, materialism, and competition can leave us feeling disconnected, anxious, and insecure. Kindness, which the Buddhists call compassion, can restore our peace of mind by bringing us a sense of connection with all living things (Mingyur Rinpoche, 2007). I use the words *kindness* and *compassion* interchangeably. The Dalai Lama (1995) says that his religion is kindness, and he sees compassion as not only a natural human tendency but also the path to personal and planetary peace.

In our challenging world today, we need compassion more than ever. To find out more about how to cultivate it, I interviewed Dr. James Doty, neurosurgeon and founder of Stanford University's Center for Compassion and Altruism Research and Education (CCARE). Wearing bright green scrubs and greeting me with a warm smile, Dr. Doty ushered me into his office filled with books, models of the brain, Tibetan prayer flags, and pictures with the Dalai Lama (Doty, J. R. Personal communication, July 10, 2019).

One reason we're feeling so stressed and disconnected, Dr. Doty told me, is that contemporary culture works against our natural rhythms. We're deprived of sleep by electric lights and electronic communication, assaulted by workplace demands, and exhausted by the frantic pace of modern living, all of which can bring us chronic stress

We're also stressed by our political culture. "Unfortunately," Dr. Doty said, "we know that you can manipulate people by creating fear, whether it's a real or created fear. What happens is that it shuts down the normal mechanisms of connection," putting us into survival mode.

Yet, we can reverse this distressing trend. According to Dr. Doty, compassion makes us feel happier by stimulating the reward centers in our brains. Research at Stanford's CCARE has found that mindfully cultivating compassion can improve our health, both personally and collectively, reconnecting us to ourselves and restoring our connection with others (Jazaieri et al., 2013; Jazaieri et al., 2018). Living with compassion can transform the way you see the world. You can relate to the world with more love and less fear (Jampolsky, 2004). You'll avoid divisive gossip and social media that encourages you to compare yourself to others and compete for approval.

Living with compassion means recognizing when you're judging yourself and others or harboring resentment, which plunges you into a separate, disconnected self. You can then take a few deep, mindful breaths to expand your awareness, realizing that we are all here to learn, love, and realize our personal uniqueness and greater connectedness.

Research has found that kindness can improve your health, strengthening your immune system. (Rein et al., 1995). A review of over a hundred studies worldwide has shown that when people are kind, they feel more connected to others, experiencing greater joy, meaning, better physical health, and less anxiety and depression (Hiu et al., 2020).

Practicing compassion through acts of kindness is not only good for you, but good for those around you, helping to restore trust, cooperation, and supportive connections in your community. Neuroscience research shows that reaching out with kindness will transform our brains, making us more resilient by taking us out of isolation into relationship, making both the giver and receiver feel more cared for, connected, and secure (L. Miller et al., 2021).

One example of the power of kindness is the work of Tom Tait, when he was mayor of Anaheim, California. Believing that a city, like a person, can be healed by kindness, he cultivated a culture of kindness in his community. He began by asking elementary school children to perform a million random acts of kindness—small actions such as holding a door open for someone, giving a compliment, or planting trees to give back to Mother Nature. Mayor Tait's campaign created a kinder, more connected community. He then founded cityofkindness.org and has worked with other mayors throughout the country to cultivate greater kindness in their own communities (Dienstman, 2019).

Studies have found that kindness is contagious, producing a positive ripple effect. It can heal disconnection, reduce the crime rate, and create a more harmonious and peaceful world (Spivak & Saunders, 2020). Research has found that not only our actions but also our *attitudes* influence those around us. Cambridge biologist Rupert Sheldrake, Ph.D., has proposed that all of humanity is united in a "morphic field," (2009) and studies have shown that we are all intrinsically connected in consciousness, part of a larger reality that includes us all (Institute of Noetic Sciences, 2024; Plonka et al., 2023).

Years ago, Albert Einstein recognized this intrinsic interconnectedness. He encouraged us to expand "our circle of compassion" to include all of nature, explaining how recognizing our oneness with creation would increase our "inner security" (Popova, 2016).

As you've made your way through this book, you've already begun cultivating greater compassion by exploring practices in the Mindful Presence and

Meditation Pathways. Mindfully pausing to take a few slow deep breaths can reduce your stress level, helping you relax and respond more compassionately (Jinpa, 2015), and meditation to settle the mind is a vital part of Stanford CCARE's compassion cultivation training (Jazaieri et al., 2013).

This week, you'll learn more compassion-building practices and discover how to cultivate greater compassion for yourself and others with a loving kindness meditation. You'll explore ways to expand your circle of compassion and awaken yourself and those around you to our intrinsic interconnectedness.

Exercise: Setting Your Intention

Now it's time to set your intention for this week. (For example, "My intention is live with greater kindness.")

It's important to write down this intention as an invitation to yourself. You can record it here or in your journal.

My intention is _____

Today's Date

Now take a moment to connect with your intention.

- *Take a deep breath and slowly release it.*

- *Recall a time in your life when you experienced a deep feeling of kindness—from either giving or receiving. Was this getting support from a friend, extending kindness to someone else, witnessing an act of kindness, or something else?*

As you open your heart to greater kindness in the days ahead, keep this experience in mind.

Each day this week, you'll find a new practice for cultivating kindness. Try these practices one day at a time, and if one of the practices doesn't work for you, just repeat another practice. At the end of the week, as you look back and reflect on your experience, choose a favorite practice to take with you on your continuing journey to inner peace.

KINDNESS AND ELEVATION
WEEK 5, DAY 2

This week you're going to experience more mindfully what kindness looks like and feels like.

It's important to consider not only the act but also the intention. Kindness is *not* transactional—an act of giving only to get a desired reaction. When I find myself "looking for likes," on social media, waiting expectantly for people's responses to my posts, emails, or actions, I'm still caught up in ego. Acts of kindness transcend ego. Becoming "an instrument" of peace, we feel joy and oneness when we connect with another person in a kind act.

We can also feel joy and oneness when we see someone else performing an act of kindness. If you've felt this yourself, then you've experienced what psychologist Jonathan Haidt, Ph.D., (2000) has called *elevation,* the expansive feeling of joy we can feel when we witness acts of human kindness, caring, and compassion.

Haidt (2000) cites an example of elevation that happened one snowy winter morning. A young woman was riding with three young men, returning from volunteer work with their church. Their car passed a driveway where an older woman was standing with her shovel. One of the young men asked the driver to stop and let him out. The young woman thought he was getting out to go home but then saw him begin clearing the woman's driveway. Surprised and inspired, she was swept up in feelings of joy and admiration.

Research has shown that elevation opens our hearts to greater kindness and care, inspiring us to follow the example of the people we admire (Algoe & Haidt, 2009). Suddenly, we gain an expansive awareness that we're all connected in a larger vision of kindness, compassion, and hope.

Exercise: Kindness and Elevation

For today's practice, think of a time when you saw someone performing an act of kindness or compassion for someone else. This could be an actual experience, something you read about, or something you saw in a movie, video, or on the news. Recall the experience, when it happened, and how it made you feel.

Then, write down your experience here or in your journal.

****

Elevation Practice: _____

                                Date

Who was this kind person?

_____

What did they do?

_____

_____

What do you admire about them?

_____

How do you feel when you recall this experience?

_____

_____

PERFORMING SMALL ACTS OF KINDNESS
WEEK 5, DAY 3

In a world divided by post-pandemic change and political polarization, too many of us can feel isolated, abandoned, and alone. Psychologist Sonja Lyubomirsky, Ph.D., (2007) has found that being kind to another person can satisfy our basic need for connection and create a wave of kindness all around us.

She experienced the effects of kindness herself while standing in line at the grocery store. Hearing the young man in front of her saying he was $1.15 short of cash to pay for his food, she offered him the $1.15, then felt a rush of joyous exhilaration, and he thanked her enthusiastically.

Small acts of kindness like these can spread. For when Lyubomirsky (2007) left the store, she saw the same young man in the parking lot, helping a woman in a wheelchair lift her groceries into her car.

When we connect with others through small acts of kindness, we can cultivate connection and community while becoming happier and healthier ourselves. In fact, researcher Allan Luks (2001) found that people who help others are ten times more likely to be in good health.

Studies have shown that when we perform 3-5 small acts of kindness in one day, we can experience reduced anxiety and depression as well as major increases in well-being, life satisfaction, and social connection (Lyubomirsky et al, 2005; Cregg & Cheavens, 2022). We can experience similar results when we spread our small acts of kindness over a week (Otake et al., 2006).

Exercise: Performing Small Acts of Kindness

Today, you can choose to practice three or more small acts of kindness. Remember, these are small acts, just holding the door open for someone, saying a kind word, sending a kind note, text, or email, listening mindfully to a friend, or doing something else in the spirit of kindness and care.

Then, write down your experience here or in your journal.

****

Small Acts of Kindness Practice: _____

                                          Date

What did you do?

_____

When did you do these kind acts?

_____

What was your experience?

_____

_____

LOVING KINDNESS MEDITATION
WEEK 5, DAY 4

Today, you will learn to cultivate greater compassion with the Loving Kindness Meditation. But first, a definition. Many people confuse compassion with empathy, which means sharing the feelings of others, but these reactions are actually quite different. Empathy alone for someone in distress can lead to feelings of stress, overwhelm, and burnout. By contrast, compassion involves active commitment, kindness, and support, bringing feelings of warmth, caring, and concern for the other person together with a desire to contribute to their well-being (Singer & Klimecki, 2014).

The Loving Kindness Meditation is a simple, powerful practice to promote greater compassion for ourselves and others. In a short study at Stanford University, people meditated and sent feelings of loving kindness to two people they loved, wishing them health, happiness, and well-being. Then, they sent loving kindness to an unknown stranger. In only seven minutes, this practice increased their feelings of social connection and positivity (Hutcherson et al., 2008).

In longer studies, when people practiced the Loving Kindness Meditation for two weeks or more, they experienced greater altruism, connection, and compassion for others as well as greater mindfulness, purpose, social support, better health, and even positive changes in their brains (Fredrickson et al., 2008; Weng et al., 2013).

There are many versions of the Loving Kindness Meditation. The traditional approach, drawn from Buddhism, begins with sending loving kindness to ourselves, then to loved ones, and then to all beings, realizing that we all share the desire for happiness and relief from suffering (Mingyur Rinpoche, 2007).

However, many people in the West are caught up in inner criticism and don't feel loving acceptance of themselves. When meditation teacher Sharon Salzberg told this to the Dalai Lama, he was stunned because he'd always believed that people would naturally care for themselves (Goleman & Davidson, 2017).

Because of this self-critical attitude, many Western approaches to the Loving Kindness Meditation begin by asking us to first visualize a loved one—a family member, friend, or even a beloved pet—with loving kindness. Next, we can expand that loving kindness to include ourselves. We can then extend loving kindness to others we know and finally reach out in expansive feelings of compassion for all beings.

Here is the Loving Kindness Meditation that I use. If you are not comfortable starting with yourself, you may choose to focus on a loved one first and then on yourself, whatever works best for you.

Exercise: Loving Kindness Meditation.

To practice Loving Kindness, first take a deep, mindful breath and slowly release it.

Then say to yourself:

"May I be filled with loving kindness. May I be safe. May I be well. May I be peaceful and at ease. May I be guided by the light. May I be happy."

Next, think of someone you love—a dear friend, family member, or pet and say:

"May you be filled with loving kindness. May you be safe. May you be well. May you be peaceful and at ease. May you be guided by the light. May you be happy."

Then let your meditation expand to everyone you know and all beings on this planet, saying:

"May we all be filled with loving kindness. May we be safe. May we be well. May we be peaceful and at ease. May we be guided by the light. May we be happy."

Then, write down your experience here or in your journal.

****

Loving Kindness Meditation: _____

                                                    Date

When did you do this meditation?

_____

_____

What was your experience?

_____

_____

SELF-COMPASSION
WEEK 5, DAY 5

I grew up with a strong sense of duty and discipline. On Saturday mornings, I'd do my household chores—dust and vacuum, clean the kitchen and bathrooms, polish the furniture, and other tasks.

One Saturday afternoon, after finishing my chores, I went out to the patio to relax with a favorite book, when my mother came out and said, "Don't just sit there. Do something useful. Go pull weeds on the hill." So, after that, every Saturday, for hours, I'd pull weeds on the rocky hillside in the hot afternoon sun.

Years later, I realized that I'd brought this old pattern with me—subordinating myself to endless tasks. I'd tell myself I could relax and do what I wanted *only* after I got all the work done. I needed to learn to be kinder to myself, to treat myself like a good friend. As Buddhist teacher Yongey Mingyur Rinpoche says (2007, p. 250), practicing compassion for all beings means "ending an abusive relationship with yourself."

Psychologist Kristin Neff, Ph.D. (2011) recommends a three-step practice to cultivate greater self-compassion. You can use this practice whenever you're caught up in endless striving or feeling worried, anxious, or self-critical. To do this, you'll first mindfully acknowledge what you're feeling, then realize that it's only human to experience these feelings, and finally, comfort yourself as you would a dear friend.

Exercise: Self-Compassion Practice

Try this self-compassion practice:

- ***Mindfulness.*** *Instead of attacking or shaming yourself, tune in to how you feel. Ask "What am I feeling?" and name your feelings, whatever they might be. For example, "I feel sad. . . scared. . . anxious. . .ashamed. . .hurt. . . angry. . . worried. . ." or something else.*

- ***Common humanity.*** *Remind yourself that it's only human to feel this way. Tell yourself, "It's OK. No one's perfect."*

- ***Kindness to yourself.*** *Actively soothe yourself with kind words. You can put your hand on your heart if you like and reassure yourself by saying something like, "I know this is hard and you're really hurting right now. I'm here for you" (Neff, 2011, pp. 103-104).*

If you'd like further information on the Self-Compassion practice, see https://self-compassion.org/self-compassion-practices/

When you've done the Self-Compassion practice, write down your experience here or in your journal.

****

Self-Compassion Practice: _____

Date

When did you do this practice?

_____

What was your experience? _____

RELEASING RESENTMENT
WEEK 5, DAY 6

In our journey from childhood to adulthood, many of us had someone hurt or disappoint us, leaving us feeling sad, angry, and resentful. Some of us grew up in dysfunctional families or had loved ones who left us, friends who let us down, or a hostile work environment.

You may have known people who tried to control you, lashing out in anger if they didn't get their way. Living with kindness does *not* mean subjecting yourself to continuing abusive situations. If you have an abusive person in your life, professional counseling can help you learn to set boundaries and navigate your way to healthier relationships.

Being kind to yourself can involve letting go of a relationship that brings you distress. It can also mean releasing any remaining resentment. Even if your hurtful relationship was years ago, that person could still be emotionally present for you. As my friend Pat says, "Are they still occupying your mind without paying rent?"

Whatever the cause, releasing resentment can be an act of kindness toward yourself. Research has shown that holding a grudge can produce chronic stress, which can undermine your health (T. Q. Miller et al., 1996; Tennen & Affleck, 1990; Worthington, & Scherer, 2004).

Trying to deny your hurt feelings doesn't help either because painful feelings can become locked in our bodies, causing physical and emotional distress (van der Kolk, 2015). Underlying resentment could be casting a shadow on your current relationships, interfering with your ability to trust and connect with the people in your life. In this case, releasing resentment is a kindness not only to yourself but to those around you.

Psychologist Fred Luskin, Ph.D., is the founder of the Stanford Forgiveness Project that helps people learn to release resentment and conducts research on the health benefits of forgiveness. Luskin says that forgiveness is primarily for us—to free ourselves from painful resentment and restore our peace of mind. His research (1999; 2002) shows that people who completed the Forgiveness Project experienced decreased stress and better health.

According to Luskin, forgiveness does *not* mean excusing, denying, or forgetting the offense. It may not even mean reconciling with the other person. What it *does* involve is recognition and positive action: recognizing when you're feeling distressed, whether the offense was ten minutes or ten years ago, then taking positive action to regain your peace of mind (2002; Marsh 2010).

Exercise: Releasing Resentment

Do you feel resentment for someone who has hurt or disappointed you? To release a serious abusive relationship, you may need the support of a compassionate therapist or other helping professional. Otherwise, try this simple practice of recognition and release.

1. *First, focus on how you feel when you think of this person and situation If you've been denying your negative feelings, take a deep mindful breath and ask yourself, "When I think of _____, what do I feel? For example, do I feel: upset, angry, anxious, hurt, sad, heartbroken, rejected, miserable, or something else?*

2. *When you think about what happened, tell yourself that what they did was <u>not</u> OK.*

3. *Give yourself self-compassion, acknowledging that it's only human to feel upset about this. Console yourself with kind words as you would comfort a dear friend.*

4. *Reach out for support. Share what happened with someone you trust. Can you learn something from the experience that can help you in the future?*

5. *Realize that you have the power to choose, to shift your focus. Think of an experience that brings you joy. For example, connect with the beauty of nature, listen to your favorite music, or participate in an activity you enjoy. You <u>do</u> have a choice.*

6. *If you're ready to release your resentment to gain greater peace of mind, take a long deep breath and slowly release it. Then say a short affirmation of release. Perhaps you could say, "I now let go of resentment for _____ (this person). Or you could say, "I bless you and release you to your highest good." Releasing or loosening resentment is a kindness to ourselves. In the Jewish tradition (Berns-Zare & Hayman, 2022) the act of blessing others blesses us as well.*

7. *Expand your perspective. Life is a mixture of sunlight and shadow. Despite the shadows of the past, you can also feel joy for the light in your life today.*

Write down your experience here or in your journal.

****

Releasing Resentment Practice: _____

                                       Date

When did you do this practice?

_____

What was your experience?

_____

REFLECT AND REVIEW
WEEK 5, DAY 7

This week, you were invited to try these practices:

1. Kindness and Elevation

2. Performing Small Acts of Kindness

3. Loving Kindness

4. Self-Compassion

5. Releasing Resentment

As you look back on your week, reflect on your responses. Review how each practice made you feel, and choose at least one practice you'd like to take along on your journey to greater peace of mind. Then write down your experience here or in your journal

****

Week 5 Review: _____

Date

What practice would you like to take with you?

_____

What feelings does this practice inspire for you?

_____

How can you use this practice to develop greater peace of mind in the days to come?

_____

CHAPTER 6

The Path of Purpose

PREPARATION
WEEK 6, DAY 1

Having a sense of purpose can connect us to something larger than ourselves, bringing us greater vitality, hope, and wellbeing (Aftab, 2020; McKnight & Kashdan, 2009).

Yet today, too many of us lack a sense of purpose. According to research, two thirds of Americans are focused only on our daily needs and obligations (Kobau et al., 2010). Without purpose, we're missing a powerful source of connection in our lives. And recent research has found a vital link between purpose, health, and hope (Graham, 2023, p. 30). By finding a sense of purpose, we can build greater hope for our future, both individually and collectively.

As psychiatrist Viktor Frankl, MD, realized, having a sense of purpose not only brings us hope but can improve our health and even save our lives. As a prisoner in the Nazi concentration camp of Auschwitz, he saw how people survived when they had something to live for, while those who had lost hope succumbed to the camp's brutal conditions. Frankl's book manuscript was confiscated when he entered Auschwitz. But throughout his daily trials and deprivations, he wrote notes on scraps of paper, determined to finish his book. As he later explained in *Man's Search for Meaning*, this commitment brought him a sense of purpose and the hope to survive (1959/1984, pp. 126-127). Research has now shown that having a sense of purpose when dealing with challenges can reduce stress-induced anxiety, rumination, and inflammation, bringing us a greater sense of hope and control in our lives (Lachman & Schloski, 2024; Ostafin & Proulx, 2023).

In your own life today, your purpose will evolve as you mature and grow, for as research has shown, maturing involves contributing to a sphere of activity beyond our individual selves (Ryff, 1989). According to psychologist Abraham Maslow, Ph.D. (1971), we have a hierarchy of needs, from basic survival—air, water, food, and shelter—to our needs for safety, love and belonging, personal growth, self-actualization, and service to the larger community. As you move from childhood through adulthood, your purpose will expand from learning basic skills in school to developing relationships, finding meaningful work to serve your community, and later discovering new purpose and meaning in retirement.

You can discover a sense of purpose in many ways. Psychologist Todd Kashdan, Ph.D. (2009), has found that some people find their purpose by following their curiosity. Other people discover a new sense of purpose when dealing with challenges and hardships. Buddhist teacher Thich Nhat Hanh (1988, p. 30) has described how suffering can expand our awareness, and psychologist Steve Taylor, Ph.D., (2023) has found that we can be transformed through struggle. My friend, psychologist David Feldman, Ph.D., has done research on "super survivors." These people who thrive in response to life-changing trauma develop what he calls "grounded hope" (Feldman & Kravitz, 2014).

A few years ago, Dave and I met Kathryn Goetzke, whose search for hope began with a personal tragedy (Dreher, 2022; Goetzke, 2022). When Kathryn was 18, her father died. He had been her hero, her role model who loved and encouraged her. But he struggled, and Kathryn spent her young life trying to make him happy and proud. Then, suddenly, he was gone. One cold February morning during her first year of college, she called home, only to learn that her father had died by suicide.

For years, she felt guilty, spiraling into her own state of hopelessness, attempting suicide herself. Then, she turned her pain into purpose. She was told she was at high risk of suicide, yet she knew the current prevention methods would not work for her. Seeking to understand suicide and its causes, she began doing extensive research, learning that the major predictor of suicide is hopelessness. She found her purpose by discovering proven strategies to build hope and created an evidence-based Shine Hope Framework that includes teaching **S**tress Skills, **H**appiness Habits, **I**nspired Actions, **N**ourishing Networks, and **E**liminating Challenges (negative thinking patterns), practices that spell out "Shine." The more challenges a person has, the more they need to "Shine" Hope.

Kathryn shares these Shine hope skills with others in Hopeful Mindset strategies for elementary school students, teens, parents, and college students, Hopeful Workplaces, Hopeful Cities, a Hope Matrix Podcast, and other projects of her Shine Hope Company, and she's now been working with the United Nations to establish an International Day of Hope on July 12.

Connecting with a sense of purpose can help build our hope and also bring us a sense of direction in life. My research on Renaissance lives (Dreher, 2008) showed me how generations of artists, writers, scientists, and innovators found their purpose. They believed that God had given each person special gifts or talents and that by discovering and using their gifts they could find their calling, fulfilling their part in the divine plan. Yet even in those days, some people faced resistance in following their calling. When Michelangelo was a boy, his father would beat him whenever he caught him drawing, believing that art was a waste of time and his son should become a cloth merchant to bring money into the family. Fortunately for us all, Michelangelo persevered.

Today, discovering our gifts and following where they lead still inspires people to discover their callings. As a child, Jane Goodall loved animals and told her mother that she wanted to go to Africa to study the animals there. Unlike Michelangelo's father, Jane's mother encouraged her, saying that if she worked very hard, she would find a way (Kim, 2023). Jane Goodall found her purpose studying chimpanzees in Africa, gaining world renown for her research. In her 90s, she still travels throughout the world, advocating for conservation and animal welfare.

I'm convinced that each of us is here to fulfill our purpose in the larger pattern of life. If we feel disconnected, we can't see this. When we feel separate and isolated, instead of acknowledging our gifts, we compete with others, feeling inferior, anxious, and inadequate. Yet our purpose, as Maslow recognized, is to fulfill our own unique potential, to self-actualize. Like instruments in an orchestra, each of us is a vital part of the greater harmony of life.

If we're feeling disconnected in these challenging times, we can begin restoring our connection, both personally and collectively, by strengthening our sense of purpose. We can learn something new or deepen our spirituality. We can reach out to loved ones or volunteer for a cause we believe in, caring for our neighbors, our community, or the natural world. And as more of us renew our purpose, we can engage in what my Jewish friends call *Tikkun Olam*, the act of "repairing our world," together.

Exercise: Setting Your Intention

Now it's time to set your intention for this week. (For example, "My intention is live with greater purpose.")

It's important to write down this intention as an invitation to yourself. You can record it here or in your journal.

*My intention is*_____

Today's Date

Now take a moment to connect with your intention.

- *Take a deep breath and slowly release it.*
- *Recall a time in your life when you experienced an energizing sense of purpose, something that gave your life meaning, making you feel connected to something greater than yourself.*

As you open your heart to greater purpose in the days ahead, keep this experience in mind.

Each day this week, you'll find a new practice for discovering a sense of purpose. Try these practices one day at a time, and if one of the practices doesn't work for you, just repeat another practice. At the end of the week, as you look back and reflect on your experience, choose a favorite practice to take with you on your continuing journey to inner peace.

DISCOVERING YOUR STRENGTHS
WEEK 6, Day 2

In the Renaissance, people found their purpose by using their gifts (Dreher, 2008). Today, psychologists have rediscovered this Renaissance wisdom, realizing how we can find our purpose by discovering and using our personal strengths. In their groundbreaking international research, positive psychologists Martin Seligman, Ph.D., and Christopher Peterson, Ph.D., (2004) discovered 24 character strengths common to humankind. Each of us, they found, has five top strengths or "signature strengths." Research has shown that by using our top strengths on a regular basis, we can develop a stronger sense of purpose, becoming happier, healthier, and more successful (Seligman et al., 2005).

The 24 character strengths are creativity, curiosity, judgment, love of learning, perspective, bravery, perseverance, honesty, zest, love, kindness, social intelligence, teamwork, fairness, leadership, forgiveness, humility, prudence, self-regulation, appreciation of beauty and excellence, gratitude, hope, humor, and spirituality (Seligman & Peterson, 2004).

Exercise: Discovering Your Strengths

You can discover your personal strengths by taking the free VIA character survey at https://www.viacharacter.org/. You can also begin connecting with your strengths by recalling what you loved to do as a child or remembering a time in your life when you felt inspired and energized.

What were you doing? What did it look like and feel like? Were you:

- *Helping someone—Kindness*
- *Reaching out to live your values—Bravery*
- *Feeling lovingly connected to a dear friend or family member—Love*
- *Standing up for justice—Fairness*
- *Playing a team sport—Teamwork*
- *Feeling inspired by nature—Appreciation of beauty and excellence*
- *Working hard to achieve a goal—Perseverance*
- *Or something else?*

Today, you can identify your personal signature strengths by either reflecting on your life or taking the VIA character survey.

Then, write down your experience here or in your journal.

****

Discovering Your Strengths Practice: _____

Date

How did you discover your top five signature strengths?

_____

_____

What are they?

_____

How can you use your top strengths to make a positive difference in the days ahead?

_____

FINDING ROLE MODELS
WEEK 6, Day 3

You can also discover your purpose by learning from people you admire. I've always admired my father, Frank Dreher, who grew up as a poor boy on a small Kentucky farm during the Depression.

After his early morning paper route and school, Frank would spend hours out working in the fields. Late one afternoon when he saw a small plane flying overhead, he put down his tools and began running. He knew that pilots would give a boy a quarter to help tie their plane down, and a quarter was a lot of money to a poor boy during the Depression.

When Frank reached the local landing strip, a bright yellow biplane had just touched down. Inspired by its power and freedom, he just knew he had to fly. So, each day, after delivering papers and going to school, he'd return to the airport, helping the pilots tie down their planes, wash, and refuel them. Sometimes, they even took him up on short flights.

There were arguments with his mother, a devout Catholic who wanted Frank to become a priest. She nagged him constantly, insisting that he obey her and give up his crazy plans to fly. When all of this became too much, he moved into the attic of the Louisville Flying Service, where the old barnstormers and World War I pilots adopted him as one of their own.

With hardly any money, each evening he'd eat his main meal, a bowl of bean soup with lots of crackers at the airport coffee shop. He did odd jobs around the airport and persevered to follow his dream. At age sixteen, he got his pilot's license and was featured in the *Louisville Courier-Journal* as the youngest pilot in Kentucky (Dreher, 2000, pp. 26-28).

My father became a flight instructor, a pilot during World War II, and an Air Force colonel who flew jets and air rescue helicopters. I've always admired him for his courage to soar above traditional expectations to follow his dreams.

In addition to learning from people we know, research has shown that we can discover our sense of purpose from virtual role models in books and movies

(Oman & Thoresen, 2003). When I was growing up, my family moved every year or two, across the country and around the world for my father's Air Force assignments. At each new base, I'd find my way to the local library where I met virtual friends and role models in the world of books.

As a high school student, I was inspired by Eleanor Roosevelt's autobiography. I read how she overcame an emotionally abusive mother, an alcoholic father, childhood adversity, and the deaths of both parents. Turning her pain into purpose, she developed compassion and courage, standing up for justice and helping those less fortunate. Eleanor Roosevelt became a powerful role model for me. In fact, as I write this chapter, she smiles down at me from her picture on my desk.

Exercise: Finding Role Models.

Now it's your turn. Take a moment to look back on your life and remember someone who has been an important role model for you.

- *Was this someone you knew or someone you learned about in books, in movies, or on the news?*

- *Did you admire this person for courage, compassion, resilience, or something else?*

Write down your experience here or in your journal.

****

Finding Role Models Practice: _____

                                                Date

An important role model in my life is

_____

I admire them for

_____

I want to develop more of their strength of

_____

REACHING OUT WITH PURPOSE
WEEK 6, Day 4

In his poem, "The Road Not Taken," Robert Frost writes of coming to a crossroads and taking the road that made a major difference in his life (1916/2024).

A choice can make a major difference in *our own* lives as well. Can you recall a time when you made a choice that taught you an important lesson or opened up new possibilities?

In the spring of my senior year in high school, I was almost expelled because of a choice I made.

I grew up on Air Force bases, learning military discipline, and I was expected to follow orders. As a young child, each day at sunset I had to stop playing while the bugle played *Taps*. In this daily ritual, as the American flag was lowered, all the military men and women stood at attention and saluted. I stood at attention, too, with my right hand over my heart.

When I was 16, my father was stationed in Germany, where I spent my junior and senior years at Kaiserslautern American High School. I was a shy teenager who dutifully did my chores and spent lots of time reading books—histories, novels, and biographies that opened doors to other worlds.

In my senior year, I was one of the honor students, who worked for an hour in the school office instead of going to study hall. My duties included office work and calling students in to see the principal for disciplinary action whenever they broke the rules. Our military high school had very strict rules. I'd often have to call Mike Carney out of Miss Ackerman's second period English class for joking in class, and even wearing his shirt tail out.

I didn't have a boyfriend, but I knew that Mike and Cindi were a couple. They'd see each other mainly at school, because she took the bus to school from Ramstein Air Force Base, while Mike commuted by train from Pirmasens Army Base, where his father was stationed. Each day they ate lunch together and sat together smiling during school assemblies.

One morning, when I reported to the school office, I saw Cindi slumped in a chair, her eyes red and swollen. The secretary told me that Cindi's two brothers were home recovering from the measles. Worse yet, the whole family was being air evacuated back to the States the next day because her mother had cancer. My assignment was to help Cindi clean out their lockers and check in their books before her father picked her up that afternoon.

Mumbling "I'm sorry," I walked with Cindi to her locker and we retrieved her books. On our way to her brothers' lockers, we passed Miss Ackerman's classroom. I paused, knowing that Mike was inside.

What happened next surprised me. I took a deep breath. Then, knowing this was against all the rules, I opened the door and announced, "Will Mike Carney please come to the office?" When he came out, I said, "I'm supposed to help Cindi check out of school, but I think she needs your help more than mine." He put his arm around her, and they walked down the long dark hallway to say goodbye.

After checking in all the books, Cindi and Mike spent the rest of the day together until her father returned at 3pm. I went home that afternoon with a sense of sadness, compassion, and foreboding.

The next day, the principal called me into his office and told me I had committed "a very serious offense." Because of this, I could be expelled from school and never receive my high school diploma. I stood there in silence, afraid of being expelled but feeling in my heart that what I'd done was not wrong at all.

After I promised this would never happen again, the principal said he wouldn't expel me this time because of my strong academic record, but if I ever broke the rules like this again, I'd be expelled. Then he dismissed me from the office. I spent second period in study hall for the last two months of the year.

This experience remained my secret. I never told my parents. I couldn't have explained it and didn't think they'd understand. But somehow, I knew that beyond the rigid rules of this principal there was the deeper *principle* of compassion, of giving Mike and Cindi the chance to say goodbye (Dreher, 1998).

Looking back now, I realize that the choice I made that day gave me a new sense of purpose and transformed how I saw myself and my life.

Exercise: Reaching Out with Purpose

Now it's your turn. Can you recall a time that you made a choice that made a transformative difference in your life?

What you did could have been public or private, a large act or small. Perhaps others witnessed your action. Perhaps no one else knew what you did.

- *Did you choose to live one of your strengths?*
- *Did you discover a new sense of purpose?*
- *If so, what did you learn?*

Perhaps only you will know what it meant to you, but this choice helped make you who you are.

Write down your experience here or in your journal.

****

Reaching Out with Purpose: _____

                                        Date

What did you do?

_____

Why did you do it?

_____

What strength(s) did you affirm?

_____

TAKING COLLECTIVE ACTION
WEEK 6, Day 5

Lately, national politics has become so polarized that many people have lost faith in government. But politics is not just something that happens nationally. It happens whenever people come together to listen, learn, and work together to find new solutions to our problems.

A few years ago, my neighborhood came together to stop a tall bridge from being built behind our neighbor Elaine's house. The people who proposed the bridge meant well. They wanted the bridge to take children across our local creek to University Avenue, where the town was building a new playground. But the project would be intrusive. It would remove the trees around Elaine's back yard, and when people walked across the bridge, they'd be able to look into her bedroom window.

I met with my neighbors and brainstormed, trying to find a better way for people to walk from one side of the creek to the other. And there was.

One night we all went to the Town Council meeting to present our plan— an alternative that was less intrusive, less expensive, and much safer. In the original plan, the children would walk across the bridge and end up on busy University Avenue, with its industrial buildings, heavy traffic, and no sidewalks, putting them at risk of being hit by cars.

We proposed that instead of building the bridge, the town should put sidewalks on University Avenue. Then the children could walk up to University Avenue on the sidewalk by the street beside our houses and take the new University Avenue sidewalk to the park.

When the council members accepted our plan, we applauded. Leaving the meeting, we happily high-fived each other with a sense of celebration, connection, and community.

Taking collective action can promote positive change. As I've learned from working with my neighbors, even if our actions don't always produce the outcome we want, the collective effort itself is valuable.

Taking action together to promote positive change is good for us as well as good for our communities. Research has shown that it empowers us with a shared sense of purpose and brings us greater vitality, health, and well-being (Cohen, 2022; Klar & Kasser, 2009).

EXERCISE: Taking Collective Action

Can you recall a time when you experienced a sense of purpose by taking collective action. This could be:

- *working on a team to achieve a common goal;*
- *joining with neighbors in a community project;*
- *volunteering for a cause you believe in; or*
- *something else.*

If so, write down your experience here or in your journal.

****

Collective Action and Purpose: _____

                                                              Date

What did you do and who did you do it with?

_____

_____

What was the result?

_____

Can you take collective action to make a positive difference today? If so, what is your next step?

_____

TURNING FROM PAIN TO PURPOSE
WEEK 6, Day 6

In recent years, many of us have experienced major losses. There have been losses from COVID, loss of loved ones, jobs and community, as well as losses from accidents, illness, crime, war, and natural disasters. Like earthquakes, these traumatic events can shatter the secure foundations of our lives, leaving us feeling anxious, insecure, and profoundly disconnected.

It takes time to process such losses, to deal with all the grief and changes. Yet, this process can bring us a new sense of purpose. Psychologists Richard Tedeschi, Ph.D., and Lawrence Calhoun, Ph.D., (2004) have found that people can respond to loss with the personal transformation and positive change known as "posttraumatic growth."

Deepening our compassion, spirituality, and appreciation for life, posttraumatic growth can dramatically change the way we see the world. There was the world we once knew and a new world where we discover a renewed sense of ourselves.

Responding with posttraumatic growth when her daughter was killed by a drunk driver, Candy Lightner founded Mothers Against Drunk Driving. After the mass shooting at Marjory Stoneman Douglas High School in Florida, David Hogg joined with classmates to found March for Our Lives, a national movement for saner gun laws. David Kessler, Ph.D., (2019), who lost his mother when he was a child, found his purpose helping others deal with grief and loss and now counsels grieving people and also works with physicians, nurses, counselors, and first responders in times of trauma. As you read earlier, Kathryn Goetzke (2022) responded to the pain of her father's suicide by discovering and sharing hope-building strategies with others.

When my husband Bob died, my first response was disbelief. I still expected him to walk in the door, greeting me with his warm smile, upbeat sense of humor, and colorful Brooklyn accent. Bob had long been a vital part of my life. We did research together and explored California beaches and ski slopes, New Mexico adobes, New York City, and Thoreau's Walden Pond. He published major neuroscience research and as a psychology professor was a leader at our university, where we worked together to promote greater justice and inclusiveness.

To continue our partnership and connect with a new sense of purpose, I'm writing this book and dedicating it to Bob. My goal is that for all of us who've gone through the darkness of loss, the strategies in *Pathways to Inner Peace* can renew the light of connection and hope in our lives.

Exercise: Turning from Pain to Purpose

Have you experienced major loss in your life? It could be loss of a loved one, loss of a job, loss of a beloved pet, loss of a home, or loss of something else you value.

In addition to grieving the loss, you can begin turning your pain into purpose by finding a way to honor who or what you've lost.

A first step might be to share your experience with a trusted friend or counselor. Then you can look for a way to respond with a new sense of purpose.

If you are experiencing deep grief and depression, I encourage you to seek professional help. If you are ready to begin turning pain into purpose, write your experience here or in your journal.

****

Turning from Pain to Purpose: _____

                                        Date

What is your loss?

_____

_____

Can you begin responding to this loss with greater purpose? If so, how?

_____

What is your next step?

_____

REFLECT AND REVIEW
WEEK 6, DAY 7

This week, you were invited to try these practices:

1. Discovering Your Strengths

2. Finding Role Models

3. Reaching Out with Purpose

4. Taking Collective Action

5. Turning from Pain to Purpose

As you look back on your week, reflect on your responses. Review how each practice made you feel, and choose at least one practice you'd like to take along on your journey to greater peace of mind. Write down your experience here or in your journal.

****

Week 6 Review:_____

Date

What practice would you like to take with you?

_____

What feelings does this practice inspire for you?

_____

_____

How can you use this practice to develop greater peace of mind in the days to come?

_____

_____

CHAPTER 7

The Path of Intuition and Inspiration

PREPARATION
WEEK 7, DAY 1

You know more than you think you know.

If you've had a flash of insight, experienced a remarkable coincidence, or felt immediate empathy with someone, then you've connected with your intuitive wisdom. Connecting with our intuitive source of wisdom is especially important today when we can be misled by so much unreliable information from cable news, social media, political propaganda, and conspiracy theories.

Throughout history, people have received intuitive guidance, inspiration, and information that they could not have known rationally. Researchers call these experiences "an intuitive interconnected relationship with the surrounding world that is not limited by space and time" (Wahbeh et al., 2022, pp, 3-4).

Intuitive wisdom has led to new discoveries in the arts and sciences. When Marcel Proust ate a French sugar cookie, he had a vision that inspired his novel, *À la Recherche du Temps Perdu*. Organic chemist August Kekulé's daydream of a snake biting its tail revealed the molecular structure of the benzene ring. When Elias Howe awakened at four a.m. from a dream of warriors carrying spears pierced at the top, he rushed to his workshop to invent the pierced needle for the lockstitch sewing machine.

There have been many explanations for intuition and inspiration, dating back thousands of years. In classical times, Plotinus affirmed a vision of universal oneness. Renaissance philosophers taught about the deep interconnectedness of all creation, and mystics from all spiritual traditions have experienced a sense of union with a deeper reality (Underhill, 1915; E. L. Mayer, 2007).

Recently, science has offered psychological explanations for intuitive insights. Dutch researchers have found that people make better choices about a complex decision when they consider the alternatives, then "sleep on it," which enables their unconscious minds to reveal the best solution (Dijksterhuis et al., 2006).

According to British psychiatrist Iain McGilchrist, MD, (2009), our intuitive insights come from our brain's right hemisphere, which perceives a vision of wholeness. Swiss psychiatrist Carl Jung, MD, (1964, 1997) affirmed a more spiritual approach, pointing to meaningful coincidences or "synchronicities" as evidence of the universal unconscious which connects us all.

Scientists have proposed that we share a "unified field" of consciousness (Dossey, 2013; McTaggart, 2008). British biologist Rupert Sheldrake, Ph.D., (2011) has explained that humans and animals share telepathic bonds in what he calls *morphic fields*. The 2022 Nobel Prize in physics was awarded for research on *quantum entanglement,* recognizing the interconnectedness of experience on a microscopic level (Billings, 2022).

When American astronaut Edgar Mitchell was on his mission to the moon in 1971, he looked out at our small blue planet surrounded by the black vastness of space and felt "an overwhelming sense of universal *connectedness"* (2008, p. 16). He also conducted telepathy experiments, sending random symbols and numbers to his colleagues back on earth, and they received his messages with amazing accuracy (2008, p. 77).

Returning from space, Mitchell devoted the rest of his life to exploring our universal connectedness, founding the Institute of Noetic Sciences (IONS). "Noetic," from the Greek word, *noësis,* means "inner wisdom, direct knowing, intuition, or implicit understanding" (Wahbeh et al., 2022, p. 1).

Research has shown that this inner wisdom is available to us all. Studies at IONS have revealed that 94% of Americans have had at least one experience of intuition and inspiration (Wahbeh et al., 2018).

This week we will explore ways you can become more aware of your own intuitive wisdom.

Exercise: Setting Your Intention.

Now it's time to set your intention for this week. (For example, "My intention is to become more aware of my intuitive wisdom.") It's important to write down this intention as an invitation to yourself. You can record it here or in your journal.

My intention is _____

Today's Date

Now take a moment to connect with your intention.

- *Take a deep breath and slowly release it.*
- *Recall a time in your life when you experienced intuitive awareness— perhaps a flash of insight, an immediate sense of empathy, or a sense of "knowing" beyond rational thought.*

As you open your heart to greater intuition and inspiration in the days to come, keep this experience in mind.

Each day this week, you'll find a new practice to help you become more aware of your intuitive wisdom. Try these practices one day at a time, and if one practice doesn't work for you, just repeat another practice. At the end of the week, look back, reflect on your experience, and choose a favorite practice to take with you on your continuing journey to greater connectedness and inner peace.

CREATIVE INSPIRATION
WEEK 7, Day 2

We are connected to a source of intuitive wisdom and inspiration. But to get there, we need to transcend the self-conscious level of our egos, the mental chatter of incessant planning and worry that often fills our minds. And we need to overcome habitual rushing and multitasking that produces chronic stress and further limits our awareness.

In our everyday ego consciousness, we can be productive, but not creative. Living out of habit, we can only see what we've become accustomed to see, do what we've been doing. We generate more of what we expect, more of the status quo.

Creativity is a magical process of inspiration that reveals new possibilities.

Like artists, scientists, and innovators throughout history, we can access our intuitive wisdom with the four-step creative process of preparation, incubation, inspiration, and verification.

1. Preparation is a period of active work. We all know what that is.

2. Incubation is stepping away from our work to do something else. For example, we can take a nap, go for a walk, spend time in nature, meditate, or do something else that takes our minds off our work.

3. Inspiration is the flash of insight, the new vision that appears when our ego gets out of the way.

4. Verification is when we return to our work, inspired by our vision to create new possibilities.

Incubation is essential to release the vision of inspiration. When we're working on a project and feel blocked, instead of pushing through resistance, the best thing we can do is detach. Thomas Edison and Albert Einstein had their own favorite ways to do this. Edison would take naps in his lab, and Einstein would go sailing. Then each of them would experience a new inspiration, discovering a creative solution to the problem they'd been working on.

Research has now shown how taking short breaks can connect us to our intuitive wisdom. Psychologists Ap Dijksterhuis and Loren Nordgren (2006) have found that our best decisions are often based on unconscious thought. HeartMath Institute research has revealed that we can connect with intuitive guidance when we slow down, calm our minds, and connect with our hearts (Childre et al., 2016). One way you can do this is by using Quick Coherence or another meditative practice you learned in chapter four.

Psychiatrist Iaian McGilchrist (2009) has explained that our brain's left hemisphere offers rational, predictable solutions, while our right hemisphere perceives more holistically, revealing intuitive wisdom. He points to the Renaissance as a time when generations of artists and scientists accessed this intuitive wisdom. Michelangelo envisioned each of his statues confined within a block of marble, then progressively chipped away the stone to release the magnificent figure within.

Exercise: Creative Inspiration.

To create a new Renaissance in your life, you can connect with your own intuitive wisdom, seeing beyond what is to what could be.

When you're feeling confused about a complex decision or blocked about the next step on a project, give your conscious mind a break. Detach.

- *Take a short break.*

- *Go out into nature like Einstein.*

- *Take a nap like Edison.*

- *Practice Quick Coherence or another short meditative practice.*

- *Or do something else.*

When you relax, new inspiration will come, often when you least expect it. Then you can move forward with new creative insight.

You can try this process of taking a short break for detachment today or recall a time in the past when you detached and experienced an intuitive inspiration. Then, write down your experience here or in your journal.

****

Creative Inspiration Practice: _____

Date

When you felt blocked or confused, how did you take a short break to detach from your work?

_____

What was your experience? Did you have a flash of insight?

_____

How did this process help you move forward with greater creativity?

_____

SYNCHRONICITY
WEEK 7, DAY 3

Have you experienced a remarkable coincidence in your life? Then you've known what psychiatrist Carl Jung (1997) described as *synchronicity*. Research has shown that developing a greater awareness of synchronicity in our lives can bring us greater peace of mind and relieve feelings of isolation, loneliness, and anxiety (Cho et al., 2009). These remarkable coincidences can reveal our participation in a meaningful universe and bring us greater hope.

I experienced synchronicity when I was 19. When my parents told me they couldn't afford to pay for college, I commuted for a year from their suburban home to the University of California, Riverside. Then, determined to take charge of my life, the next summer I began working at a temp agency and saving my money to support my college education.

Driving home from work one afternoon, I passed the *Press-Enterprise* office on 14th Street when a thought suddenly filled my mind: "I'm a writer. I should work *there*." Overcoming my shyness, I turned the car into the parking lot, walked into the newsroom, and said to a reporter, "I'm Diane Dreher. I'm a writer, and I'd like to apply for a job." He ushered me upstairs to the personnel office.

When I'd filled out the application, they told me their college intern had just given notice that morning. "Can you begin work on Monday?" they asked. I stood there in amazement. Synchronicity had connected me with the perfect job, 20 hours a week that I could work around my class schedule.

As a *Press-Enterprise* editorial intern, I worked my way through the University of California, Riverside. Paying for campus housing, tuition, and books, I enjoyed my newfound freedom. And I flourished in the creative atmosphere of the newsroom, writing reviews and entertainment copy and working alongside professional journalists who showed me what it means to be a writer (Dreher, 1998, pp. 164-165).

Exercise: Synchronicity.

Often when we persevere in the face of challenges, we can find new opportunities our conscious minds could never imagine. When we follow our hearts, our intuitive wisdom can reveal synchronicity, remarkable coincidences that can help us embrace our dreams.

Can you recall a time when you experienced synchronicity—a remarkable coincidence in your life? It could be something large or small, an unexpected connection that brought you greater hope.

If you had such an experience, write it down here or in your journal.

****

Synchronicity Practice: _____

                                    Date

When and how did you experience synchronicity?

_____

How did this experience affect your life?

CONNECTING WITH A GUIDE OR MENTOR
WEEK 7: Day 4

Sometimes, we can connect with people who help us see beyond who we are to realize who we *can be*.

In my third year of college, I met a professor who changed my life. As an English major, I signed up for a seventeenth-century literature class with Dr. Stanley Stewart.

From the first day of class I was inspired. I felt a strong sense of familiarity with the late Renaissance writers we studied--John Donne, George Herbert, John Milton, and Thomas Traherne. These poets asked questions I was asking myself—questions of meaning, purpose, and identity. I felt like I *knew* these writers. I'd never read them before, yet I felt at home in their poetry and their world.

I went to the college library, reading as much as I could about the Renaissance, including Dr. Stewart's books and articles. And I'd visit him during his office hours, asking more questions as I entered my own personal Renaissance, realizing that I wanted to become a college professor.

I was surrounded by people who discounted my dreams. My friends laughed at me. My boyfriend wanted me to marry him and drop out of school to work so he could go to grad school. My mother said I should become a flight attendant because I was "not too bright but had a nice personality."

Dr. Stewart was the first adult who really saw me, listening with kindness and understanding. He told me he'd been a first-generation college student himself and had gotten his Ph.D. at UCLA. Then, he hired me as his research assistant—I actually got paid for reading books and articles about the literature I loved.

Following my dreams, I excelled in my studies, was inducted into *Phi Beta Kappa,* and graduated from UC Riverside *summa cum laude.* With Dr. Stewart's recommendation, I received a graduate fellowship to UCLA where I got my Ph.D. in Renaissance literature. Then, I began my own career of teaching, writing, and mentoring students, gratefully passing on to others the gift Dr. Stewart had given me.

We now know from research on resilience that it takes only one supportive adult—a teacher, coach, relative, or neighbor—to help a young person develop resilience and hope. Psychologists Emmy Werner and Ruth Smith (1992) studied the lives of over 500 young people from dysfunctional families, challenged by poverty, divorce, abuse, alcoholism, and mental illness. Yet, they found that some of these young people flourished because they had *one caring adult* in their lives. An aunt, uncle, grandparent, minister, coach, neighbor, or teacher really saw them and encouraged them, helping them see beyond current conditions to believe in themselves and their future.

Exercise: Connecting with a Guide or Mentor.

Can you think of someone who brought greater hope to your life? Was there one adult who really saw you?

- *If so, was this person a favorite teacher?*
- *An aunt or uncle?*
- *A helpful neighbor?*
- *A coach or scout leader?*
- *Someone else?*

If you had such a guide or mentor, write down your experience here or in your journal.

****

Connecting with a Guide or Mentor Practice: _____

Date

When and how did you connect with your guide or mentor?

_____

_____

How did this experience affect your life?

_____

Is there a way that you can become that one caring adult for a young person in your life today?

_____

THIS OR SOMETHING BETTER
WEEK 7: Day 5

As we reach for our goals, sometimes our conscious minds can't see the larger picture. We don't know that something other than what we want could actually be better for us.

In my last year of grad school at UCLA, I applied for the Clark Library dissertation fellowship, which was awarded to the top dissertation student in seventeenth-century literature. The Clark scholar received living expenses and a private office at the Clark Memorial Library, a priceless collection of seventeenth- and eighteenth-century books.

I was writing my dissertation on the seventeenth-century poet Thomas Traherne, and was the only straight-A grad student that year, so imagine my surprise when the Clark fellowship was given to someone else. When I met with my dissertation advisor, he told me the faculty had given the Clark fellowship to Amanda, who was getting divorced. I received a smaller dissertation fellowship for research at the Huntington Library across town in San Marino.

At first, I was disappointed. The Huntington Library was a long freeway commute through downtown Los Angeles, and I'd have to finish my research by 3pm to avoid getting stuck for hours driving home in LA commute traffic. But on the plus side, the library had a wonderful collection of rare books, beautiful gardens, and a small café where I could meet other scholars.

The Huntington was only a few blocks away from my cousin Norma's apartment in Pasadena. Norma invited me to stop by for dinner if I wanted to work at the Huntington until 5pm. That way, she said, I could relax, visit with her, and leave for home when the traffic cleared.

Norma was actually my mother's cousin, more like an aunt. The only woman in our family with her own career, she was office manager at Luscombe Engineering. She was also the family eccentric, criticized by all my conservative relatives. Norma had a gold Buddha statue in her living room and shelves filled with books about meditation, yoga, and Eastern philosophy. "Mi casa, su casa," she said. Inviting me to spend the night in her guest room whenever I liked, she gave me a key to her apartment.

In addition to offering her kindness and hospitality, Norma opened my eyes to intuitive wisdom. We'd have long talks about meditation, intuition, and spirituality. She taught me how to visualize a goal, begin feeling that I'd achieved it, and then give thanks "for this or something better."

I'd gotten something better than the Clark fellowship. I found a relationship that brought me love, joy, and inspiration during my last year of grad school. I smile, recalling all the times my friends and I would gather around Norma's table for gourmet meals, sharing insights from our lives, learning and laughing together.

"This or something better." As much as I enjoyed my research at the Huntington Library, my dissertation year's greatest gift was discovering something better, an inspiring relationship with my dear cousin Norma.

Exercise: This or Something Better.

Now, look back on your own life. Was there a time you wanted one thing, were initially disappointed, and then got something better than you'd expected?

If you had such an experience, write about it here or in your journal.

****

This or Something Better Practice: _____

                                                                                    Date

What did you expect and what did you get instead?

_____

Why was this experience better and how did it affect your life?

_____

VISUALIZATION AND REALIZATION
WEEK 7: Day 6

When my grad student friends and I were finishing our dissertations, we began applying for college teaching jobs. That year the job market was terrible. There were not enough jobs for all the new Ph.D.s.

"I'd like a tenure-track job teaching Renaissance literature in the San Francisco Bay Area," I told my friends. "You're crazy," they said. "Last year our top student in Renaissance literature could only get a one-year temporary job at a small college in Texas." And my professors told me that *none* of our recent Ph.D.s had ever gotten a tenure-track job in the Bay Area.

The only one who encouraged me was Norma, who said my pessimistic friends had "no *invisible* means of support." She told me to do yoga, meditate, and visualize my goal. First, she said, I needed to clear my mind, to get the negative thoughts out of the way. This was no easy task with all the complaints around me about the job market. But she gave me a book on yoga and showed me how to meditate and visualize my goal.

Research has now confirmed Norma's approach to visualization, recognizing that clearing the mind is essential (Beauregard & O'Leary, 2007; Dossey, 2013). Mental noise, worry, guilt, and resentment can block our access to intuitive guidance. And ego-driven demands don't work either. What *does* work is meditation, which puts us into a receptive, noetic state (Garland, 2007; Wahbeh et al., 2022).

So, I took Norma's advice. Each morning I'd do some simple yoga postures and meditate, then practice visualizing my goal. Giving thanks for "this or something better" developed my belief that I was living in a meaningful universe and my life had purpose.

I also did all the practical things, sending out applications and setting up interviews at the Modern Language Association's annual conference in Chicago. That December, I shared a room at the conference hotel, the Palmer House, with another grad student. Since we couldn't afford to eat in restaurants, we bought snack food at a convenience store and hung it in a bag out our hotel room window for refrigeration.

After my interviews, I came home from Chicago, continuing my yoga, meditation, and visualization. One day, something remarkable happened. At the end of my meditation, in my mind, I saw myself standing in a classroom teaching Shakespeare as golden sunlight streamed through the windows of a building with California mission architecture. As I opened my eyes, I was filled with joy and a deep sense of peace.

A few days later, I got a phone call from Dr. Frank Duggan, the English department chair at Santa Clara University, offering me a tenure-track job teaching Renaissance literature. I accepted enthusiastically, and he invited me to visit the campus. The next week, when I flew up to the San Francisco Bay area, he met me at the airport. As we drove into campus with its beautiful mission architecture, I felt I was coming home.

Norma was right. Shakespeare knew this too. Despite all the discord in the world that he called "the slings and arrows of outrageous fortune," he also recognized that "there's a divinity that shapes our ends." (1623/1997, *Hamlet*, 3.1.60 & 5.2.10-11). When we connect with that divinity, our intuitive wisdom can light up new paths of discovery, joy, and hope.

EXERCISE: Visualization and Realization.

Take a moment to look back on your life. Was there a time you visualized a goal and achieved it?

- *If so, what was it?*
- *Was it a childhood goal?*
- *A career goal?*
- *Or something else?*

Now ask yourself, "Would I like to set a new goal and begin visualizing it now?"

Write your visualization experience here or in your journal.

****

Visualization and Realization Practice: _____

                                                                Date

Was there a time in the past when you visualized and goal and achieved it? If so, what was it?

_____

_____

What is a new goal you'd like to achieve ?

_____

How can you clear your mind of mental noise and worry?

_____

How can you visualize yourself achieving your goal?

_____

REFLECT AND REVIEW
WEEK 7, DAY 7

This week, you were invited to try these practices:

1. Creative Inspiration

2. Synchronicity

3. Connecting with Mentors and Guides

4. This or Something Better

5. Visualization and Realization

As you look back on your week, reflect on your responses. Review how each practice made you feel, and choose at least one practice you'd like to take along on your journey to greater peace of mind. Then, write down your experience here or in your journal.

****

Week 7 Review: _____

Date

What practice would you like to take with you?

_____

What feelings does this practice inspire for you?

_____

_____

How can you use this practice to develop greater peace of mind in the days
to come?

_____

_____

The Path of the Arts

PREPARATION
WEEK 8, DAY 1

Have you ever been inspired by a memorable film, concert, novel, painting, or other work of art? Then you've connected with the evocative power of the arts.

The arts offer a source of inspiration and wisdom that can touch our hearts and transform our lives. Ralph Waldo Emerson said that the arts speak a "universal language" of "purity, love, and hope" (1903. P. 252), and Thomas Merton found a powerful connection between the arts and mystical experience (1948, pp. 202-203).

When we're feeling overwhelmed by today's challenging world, we can distract ourselves by binge watching television or mindlessly scrolling through social media. Yet, research has shown that such passive forms of recreation can leave us feeling exhausted and discontent (Csikszentmihalyi, 1990, p. 163; Kaplan & Berman, 2013).

By connecting with the arts, we can experience an engaging world of greater joy, inspiration, and meaning (Winston, 2006). Transporting us beyond our separate selves, the arts offer an experience of creative engagement that takes us to other lives, other times, and other worlds.

Poetry, novels, painting, sculpture, drama, music, and dance can expand our awareness and even put us into a meditative state (Magsamen & Ross, 2023). Psychologist Mihaly Csikszentmihalyi, Ph.D., (1990) found that by connecting with the arts, we can experience flow. Transcending ego separation, we can become intrinsically connected, fully present, and one with the creative process.

According to psychologist Dacher Keltner, Ph.D, (2023) the arts can bring us into a state of awe, a mystical encounter with the vast beauty and mysteries of life. The poet William Blake expressed this expansive awareness in these memorable lines:

To see a world in a grain of sand,

And a heaven in a wild flower,

Hold infinity in the palm of your hand,

And eternity in an hour (1863/1982, p. 490).

Research has found that connecting with the arts can make us healthier, wiser, and more creative. Listening to Mozart has been linked to greater mathematical ability (J. M. Taylor & Rowe, 2012). Playing a musical instrument stimulates children's developing brains, improving their judgment, intellectual ability, and social skills (Habibi et al., 2021).

Reading fiction can build our empathy (Djikic et al., 2013), and writing about life's challenges can be highly therapeutic (Pennebaker, 1997). Visiting an art gallery can increase our wellbeing (McKeown et al., 2016), and even short periods of drawing can relieve stress, bringing us greater joy and perspective on our lives (Kaimal et al., 2016).

Participation in the arts can also awaken our intuition and inspiration, leading to greater creativity and innovation. Many successful scientists have actively participated in the arts. Albert Einstein played the violin, Carl Sagan wrote fiction, and Alexander Fleming, who discovered penicillin, was an accomplished landscape artist (Root-Bernstein et al., 2008).

Yet today, too many educational institutions are eliminating arts education to focus on standardized proficiency tests. And school libraries are banning literary classics, including *The Diary of Anne Frank* and *To Kill a Mockingbird*, books that can help us better understand ourselves, one another, and our world.

But this week, you can increase your sense of connection, creativity, joy, and wellbeing by experiencing the transformational power of the arts

Exercise: Setting Your Intention.

Now it's time to set your intention for this week. (For example, "My intention is to connect more deeply with the arts.")

It's important to write down your intention as an invitation to yourself. You can record it here or in your journal.

My intention is _____

Today's Date

Take a moment to connect with your intention.

- *Take a deep breath and slowly release it.*
- *Recall a time in your life when you experienced an inspiring connection with the arts. Was it with music, painting, fiction, poetry, drama, dance, or some other art form?*

As you open your heart to greater connection with the arts in the days ahead, keep this experience in mind.

Each day this week, you'll read about a new practice for connecting with the arts. Try these practices one day at a time, and if one practice doesn't work for you, just repeat another practice. At the end of the week, as you look back, reflect on your experience and choose a favorite practice to take with you on your continuing journey to inner peace.

LITERARY ART
WEEK 8, DAY 2

Reading literature can expand our awareness, bringing us inspiration, consolation, and a greater understanding of ourselves and one another. From literary classics to contemporary poetry, novels, memoirs, and biographies, reading these works can connect us with virtual companions who have felt what we feel when facing life's challenges.

With its vivid imagery and symbolic language, poetry can make us aware of our deeper feelings. In fact, poems are often used in therapy to help people explore their emotional memories, heal dysfunctional patterns, and renew their hope (Alfrey et al., 2021).

Reading poetry can offer consolation, helping us feel that we are not alone. One night, years ago, I was feeling depressed and confused about my life. While preparing to teach the next day, I opened my Shakespeare book to sonnet 29 (1997, pp. 1932-1933):

> *"When, in disgrace with fortune and men's eyes,*
>
> *I all alone beweep my outcast state."*

I paused in amazement, realizing that, over 400 years ago, *Shakespeare* had felt this way, too. He knew, he understood, the desolation and disconnection I was feeling.

The sonnet continued, *"Yet in these thoughts myself almost despising"* as he wrestled with the darkness of despair. Then suddenly, he thought of a dear friend, and his whole world changed:

> *". . .and then my state,*
> *Like to the lark at break of day arising*
> *From sullen earth, sings hymns at heaven's gate;*
> *For thy sweet love remembered such wealth brings,*
> *That then I scorn to change my state with kings."*

As I read the poem, I thought of my own dear friend, far away, yet always in my heart. And like the lark soaring high above the darkness, my mood changed to gratitude. Inspired, I took out my old guitar, began strumming chords, and set the sonnet to music. Singing it several times, I discovered new harmonies where I had once felt only discord and disconnection.

Like poetry, fiction can also take us from isolation to connection in books that open doors to other worlds. In my teens, I used to read novels in bed at night with a flashlight, traveling far beyond my limited self to other lives and times.

Research has found that reading is the most widely reported source of flow, a state when we transcend our limited egos, becoming completely immersed in an activity (McQuillan & Conde, 1996). Reading novels, biographies, autobiographies, and memoirs can expand our experience, inspire us, and bring us greater empathy and understanding (Nell, 1988; Djikic, et al., 2013).

In reading about the lives of others we can learn from the trials and triumphs of those who've come before us. For years, I taught a seminar on autobiography for graduating seniors who were about to begin a new chapter of their lives. I wanted my students to learn how Eleanor Roosevelt, Winston Churchill, Jane Goodall, Nelson Mandela, and others overcame disappointments and personal challenges and went on to become creative leaders who held out the light of hope for their people.

Helping us develop our own capacity to hope, inspiring lives like theirs can light the way for the rest of us.

Exercise: Literary Art.

Were you ever inspired by a work of literary art? A memorable

Novel?

Biography?

Autobiography?

Memoir?

Poem?

When did you read it?

Perhaps you'd like to revisit it this week. Or can you think of a new literary work you'd like to begin reading?

If so, write down your experience here or in your journal.

****

Literary Art Practice: _____

                                                             Date

I was inspired by _____

What inspired me was _____

This week I will [revisit this literary work that inspired me in the past or explore this new form]

_____

VISUAL ART
WEEK 8, Day 3

Since the dawn of human history, people have created visual art. The Lescaux cave paintings of animals in southwestern France date back 20,000 years.

One advantage of moving around for my father's Air Force assignments was my early exposure to art. When I was six, my father worked at the Pentagon, and I saw portraits of the presidents in the National Gallery in Washington, D.C. At the magnificent Lincoln Memorial, I discovered the power of sculpture. Years later, when my father was stationed in Germany, we visited the Louvre in Paris, where I saw Leonardo da Vinci's *Mona Lisa* with her mysterious smile. We traveled to Florence, Italy, where I stood in awe before Michelangelo's *David*.

Seeing remarkable paintings and photographs can make us more aware of the beauty around us. Ansel Adams's iconic black and white photographs of Yosemite National Park capture the immense power and grandeur of nature. In contrast, Edward Weston's close-up photographs of mushrooms and bell peppers and Georgia O'Keeffe's intimate portraits of flowers take us deep into the wonders of nature that exist right before our eyes—if we only look closely enough.

Research has shown how visual art can expand our awareness of ourselves and our possibilities. Studies at a London art gallery revealed that when people viewed works of art, they experienced greater mental health and wellbeing, feeling more calm, confident, and spiritually inspired (McKeown et al., 2016).

When I was doing my dissertation research on Renaissance writers at the Huntington Library, I'd take breaks to visit the art gallery next door where I saw Thomas Lawrence's *Pinkie*, Thomas Gainsborough's *Blue Boy*, and drawings by William Blake. Now, looking back at that time, I realize how the art inspired me to think more creatively about my life and brought me greater hope for the future.

My husband Bob was inspired by art in his teens. Growing up as a poor boy in a Brooklyn housing project, he began taking the subway into Manhattan to visit the Metropolitan Museum. Exploring the Met's rich collection of Renaissance masters, Impressionists, and modern artists expanded his vision of possibility. As a first-generation college student, he went on to get a Ph.D. in neuroscience and do research on the brain. Years later, when we visited New York, he took me to the Met, where we had a wonderful time exploring the art together.

Exercise: Visual Art.

This week, I invite you to explore the visual art of painting, photography, or sculpture.

- *You could visit an art gallery or check out a book of your favorite artist's works from your local library.*

- *You could go online to look up a favorite artist.*
- *Or you could virtually "visit" an art exhibition from the Lescaux cave paintings to the Louvre.*

Whatever you choose, take the time to mindfully reflect on the art. Then write down your experience here or in your journal.

****

Visual Arts Practice: _____

Date

I explored the art of

_____

By [visiting a gallery, reading an art book, visiting virtually online]

_____

This is what I experienced

_____

MUSICAL ART
WEEK 8, Day 4

Throughout history, music has helped people transcend feelings of disconnection, bringing new harmonies to their lives. One night Henry David Thoreau heard piano music in the distance and wrote in his journal, "At length the melody steals into my being. . . .I am attuned to the universe, . . . my being moves in a sphere of melody, my fancy and imagination are excited to an inconceivable degree" (Stapleton, 1960, p. 91).

Psychiatrists have found that music can be therapeutic and transformational. Italian psychiatrist Roberto Assagioli would prescribe marches, waltzes, and classical music to help his clients gain greater motivation and peace of mind (1973, 1976).

Music can also renew our connection with one another. British psychiatrist Iain McGilchrist, MD, found that music can bind us together, making us more aware of our shared human experience (2009, p. 104).

When I was a grad student at UCLA, my neighbors and I would spend many evenings in our apartment's laundry room, playing our guitars and singing folk songs. Making music together was a great way to relieve stress at the end of the day. As our music echoed off the bare cement walls, the effect at times was amazing, as our voices would blend together beautifully in a common chord. One night after our last song, I said, "If only more people could sing together, we'd have greater peace in the world."

Singing actually had this effect during World War I, causing an unofficial cease fire on Christmas Eve, 1914. When allied British and French soldiers and their German enemies heard each other singing carols in the trenches, they stopped shooting and began singing carols together. In some areas, soldiers from the two sides left their trenches and exchanged tins of food and holiday greetings. The truce continued for two days until the armies received strict orders from their commanding officers to resume fighting the war (Imperial War Museums, 2025).

Research has now shown that music can touch our hearts and affect us on multiple levels. It can promote greater harmony within us, connecting us with our deepest needs, goals, and dreams, and also promote greater harmony around us, leading to increased altruism and connection with others (De Leeuw et al., 2021).

Research has revealed the healing effects of music, from stress relief to improved cognitive performance and better health. Studies have found that students perform better with Mozart's music playing in the background (J.M. Taylor & Rowe, 2012). And listening to music can help relieve pain and produce cardiovascular benefits (Chandra & Levitin, 2013; McCraty et al., 1996).

Exercise: Musical Art.

This week, I invite you to experience the transformational power of music for yourself.

- *There are many forms you can explore, from vocal to instrumental versions, including classical, jazz, show tunes, folk, rock, country, and contemporary music.*
- *You could attend a concert, in person or online.*
- *Or you could listen to a recording of your favorite music.*

Whatever you choose, mindfully reflect on how you feel. Then, write down your experience here or in your journal.

****

Listening to Music Practice: _____

                                                                    Date

I explored this form of music

_____

By [attending a concert, listening to a recording]

_____

This is what I experienced

_____

DRAMATIC ART
WEEK 8, DAY 5

Dramatic art can excite our emotions and expand our imagination. There's nothing quite like live theatre to connect us with the actors and audience in a shared dramatic experience.

For many years, Bob and I would enjoy live Shakespeare performances when a local drama group set up a small Elizabethan theater each summer in the park near our house. We'd bring our picnic basket for dinners with friends and neighbors. Then, after sundown, we'd watch the young actors and faculty from the local community college perform under the stars. As they breathed life into Shakespeare's *As You Like It, Twelfth Night, Hamlet,* and other classic plays, their energy and enthusiasm touched our hearts.

The little theatre is gone now. There are no more Shakespeare performances in the park, but I smile as I recall the young actors' performances that brought our community together on those memorable summer nights.

Dramatic art can be good for us on many levels. In classical times, Aristotle described how tragedy could produce *catharsis,* relieving the audience's pent-up tension when they reacted emotionally to the characters on stage. Research has shown that dramatic comedy can also relieve our tension, as we experience joy, laughter, and relief when the characters' conflicts are resolved into new harmonies (Schaper, 1968). And drama is often used in Gestalt therapy and psychodrama when people can act out their personal conflicts, heal from past traumas, and gain greater insight into their lives (Frydman, 2016; Kedem-Tahar & Felix-Kellermann, 1996).

Watching movies can also engage our emotions and take us into other lives and times. Research in media psychology reveals how we can feel excitement and empathy as we're drawn into the characters' dilemmas, often gaining greater perspective on our own lives (Bartsch, 2012). We can also experience these emotional effects with opera and ballet, performances that combine drama with the power of music.

Exercise: Dramatic Art

This week, I invite you to experience the power of dramatic art for yourself. You could:

- *attend a play, opera or ballet;*
- *watch a movie; or*

- *reflect on a time you were inspired by an experience of dramatic art.*

Whatever you choose, write your experience here or in your journal.

****

Dramatic Art Practice: _____

                                    Date

I explored this form of dramatic art

_____

By [attending a dramatic performance, watching a movie, or reflecting on a past experience with dramatic art]

_____

This is what I experienced

_____

CREATING ART
WEEK 8, DAY 6

While we can be inspired by appreciating many art forms, actively creating our own art can also take us beyond our separate egos into new worlds of possibility.

According to meditation teacher Sharon Salzberg, creating art can be a meditative practice (Magsamen & Ross, 2023, p. 67). Psychologist Dacher Kelter, Ph.D., (2023) has found that creating art can bring us awe, a sense of connection with the vast mystery of life. And psychologist Mihaly Csikszentmihalyi, Ph.D., (1997) found that actively participating in the arts can put us into a flow state, where we transcend our sense of separation, becoming fully involved in the process.

Creating art can be tremendously healing (Block et al., 2022). Studies have shown that even short periods of performing music, making visual art, or writing about our lives can relieve stress, raise our mood, and promote greater understanding (Kaimal et al., 2016).

Creating in many mediums can bring us joy, empowerment, inspiration, and an ongoing sense of discovery. New York artist Loren Ellis not only experiences these effects for herself but has helped thousands of others discover them as well. An award-winning visual artist, Loren creates what she terms "photographic painting" to convey the dynamic harmony of nature. Loren and I connected when she contacted me in 2020 to ask me for permission to include one of my *Tao* book covers in her documentary.

In 2000, Loren founded Art for Healing NYC Int'l, a nonprofit organization. She opened her midtown Manhattan studio to her charity and the local community, inviting people to participate in the arts and experience their healing effects. Her nonprofit offered exhibition space and consultation to many local and international artists, and sponsored interactive visual and performing arts programs and classes, healing meditations, and community arts events. For over two decades (2000-2022), this visionary nonprofit received numerous grants and awards for nurturing people's lives through their involvement in the arts.

Now, in a fresh new way, Loren continues the spirit of Art for Healing NYC Int'l.org in her book, *Essence of an Artist: Follow Your Dream* (2021; 2025). Her new book was *not* Loren's idea. She tells the mystical story in the introduction. Through her award-winning book and the documentary that mirrors the book, she continues to help others experience the joy of creation. Sharing her artwork, poetry, and personal reflections, Loren Ellis encourages us all to discover the healing power of the arts for ourselves.

The healing power of the arts can take many forms. Drawing and painting have often been used in therapy to help people recover from depression, develop greater self-confidence, build their personal resources, and relate to others more effectively (Field & Kruger, 2008; Van Lith et al., 2013).

Research has shown how painting a still life or landscape can expand our perspective and improve our ability to solve problems (Diliberto-Macaluso & Stubblefield, 2015). When my colleague, engineering professor Park Chan, Ph.D., would reach an impasse in his research, he'd take a break to create beautiful Chinese paintings of mountains, flowers, and bamboo. Then, he'd return to the lab with new insights and solutions. And when British prime minister Winston Churchill faced major challenges during World War II, he found inspiration and renewed hope painting landscapes.

Making music can raise our mood, broaden our perspective, and enhance our cognitive abilities. Learning to play a musical instrument can strengthen children's developing brains, enabling them to focus their attention, develop self-discipline, think more clearly, and relate better to others (Habibi et al., 2021). Research has shown that musicians score significantly higher than non-musicians on creative thinking (Woodward & Sikes, 2015). And, as I experienced singing folk music with my neighbors long ago, singing together can foster a sense of connection and social bonding as well as relieving stress, reducing pain, and strengthening our immune systems (Beck et al., 2000; Weinstein et al., 2016).

Writing about our personal challenges can also be profoundly therapeutic. Research by Texas psychologist James Pennebaker, Ph.D., (1997) has shown that writing about a past traumatic experience for as little as 15 minutes a day over four days can change the way we organize our thoughts about the trauma and improve our emotional health. Writing about our deepest thoughts and feelings has been shown to improve our physical health as well, by relieving stress and anxiety and strengthening our immune systems, and (Pennebaker et al., 1988; Pennebaker & Segal, 1999).

We can also experience stress relief, inspiration, and empowerment by pursuing our favorite creative crafts. Research has shown how engaging in crafts such as ceramics, gardening, knitting, crocheting, weaving, quilting, and woodworking can put us into a flow state, raise our mood, and bring us greater peace of mind (Huotilainen et al., 2018; Pöllänen, 2006).

In the safe space of our creative practice, we can learn to deal more effectively with life's challenges. By seeing mistakes as part of the larger process of learning and creating, we can become more patient and resourceful. The time we spend in our practice can also help us reflect on our lives and become more mindful.

There are many ways to express our personal creativity. Some of my friends enjoy painting, calligraphy, writing poetry, dancing, singing, or playing musical instruments. And many friends have their favorite creative crafts. Tom enjoys woodworking, Tina makes beautiful quilts, Rose Marie and I enjoy making needlepoint tapestries. There's a meditative quality to the gentle rhythm of stitching, seeing the colorful yarns blend into intricate patterns. I also enjoy gardening—planting, cultivating, and watching the green plants grow in nature's evolving tapestry of life.

Exercise: Creating Art.

This week, I invite you to actively participate in an art or craft. You can reconnect with a creative practice you enjoyed in the past or explore new possibilities. You might:

- *Take that old guitar out of the closet and get reacquainted,*
- *Sign up for music lessons.*
- *Visit an art supply store.*
- *Sign up for an art or craft class at your local community center.*
- *Or do something else to express your own creative spirit.*

The choice is up to you.

Whatever you choose, write about your experience here or in your journal.

****

Creating Art Practice: _____

Date

I explored this creative practice [for example, drawing, painting, writing, singing, playing a musical instrument, pursuing the craft of_____, or something else]

_____

By [describe what you did and how]

_____

This is what I experienced

_____

REFLECT AND REVIEW
WEEK 8, DAY 7

This week, you were invited to try these practices:

1. Literary Art

2. Visual Art

3. Musical Art

4. Dramatic Art

5. Creating Art

As you look back on your week, reflect on your responses. Review how each practice made you feel, and choose at least one practice you'd like to take along on your journey to greater peace of mind. Then, write down your experience here or in your journal.

****

Week 8 Review:_____

Date

What practice would you like to take with you?

_____

What feelings does this practice inspire for you?

_____

How can you use this practice to develop greater peace of mind in the days to come?

_____

_____

CHAPTER 9

The Path of Joy

PREPARATION
WEEK 9, DAY 1

Years ago, I saw the *Declaration of Independence* at the National Archives in Washington D.C. Standing before this national treasure, I read the memorable words stating that we all have the "unalienable rights" to "life, liberty, and the pursuit of happiness." I was so inspired that I now have a framed copy of this document on the wall beside my desk.

The "pursuit of happiness" has inspired people throughout history. For centuries, the Buddhists have taught that all beings seek to find happiness and avoid suffering (Salzberg, 1995). In our own time, happiness has been extensively researched in positive psychology. As psychologist Martin Seligman, Ph.D., explains, there are two forms of happiness: the short-term pleasure we can feel eating our favorite ice cream and the deeper, more lasting joy we can find by striving for greater connection and meaning (2002, p. 9).

Psychologists call these two forms of happiness *hedonic* and *eudaimonic* (Henderson et al., 2013), but I will refer to them simply as pleasure and joy. Neuroscientist Jill Bolte Taylor, Ph.D., (2021, p. 85) has found that pleasure comes from external experiences while joy comes from deep within us. Buddhist teacher Sharon Salzberg says that joy can dissolve our sense of separateness, connecting us to all of life (1995, p. 34).

Joy opens us up to greater insight, personal growth and possibility. Psychologist Barbara Fredrickson, Ph.D. (2001, 2003) has found that the positive emotions of joy, interest, contentment, and love can broaden and build our personal resources. These emotions bring us greater emotional well-being, strengthen our attention and cognition, and increase our ability to solve problems and flourish in life. Studies have shown that cultivating positive emotions can help prevent and relieve anxiety, depression, and stress-related health problems (Fredrickson, 2002; Garland et al., 2010).

For many of us, it's been hard to feel positive lately. In recent years, our lives have been turned upside down by the COVID pandemic, political conflicts, economic uncertainty, job transitions, lost relationships, and heartbreaking wars around the world. Yet, research shows that even during troubled times, moments of joy can bring us greater meaning, resilience, and hope (Berrios et al., 2018).

But joy doesn't just happen. It must be actively cultivated. As I've learned from psychiatrist and Holocaust survivor Viktor Frankl, MD, no matter where we are, we have *the freedom to choose* our response to life. He realized, even in the desolation of a Nazi concentration camp, that everything can be taken away from us except "the last of the human freedoms—to choose one's attitude in any given set of circumstances, to choose one's own way" (1959/1984, p. 86).

Cultivating joy for us today means choosing where to focus our attention, which determines how we see the world. Lately, our attention has become a valuable commodity. Advertisers, social media entrepreneurs, and many news broadcasters seek to hijack our attention by activating our built-in negativity bias, our tendency to focus on danger and threats (Rozin & Royzman, 2001). This bias serves us well in an emergency but can keep us focused on problems, caught up in continuing worry and anxiety.

Yet, neuroscientist Jill Bolte Taylor, Ph.D., reassures us that our brain circuitry for joy is still there (2008, p. 171). We can overcome negative loops of worry, distress, and anxiety by becoming more present, more aware of opportunities for joy within and around us.

This week, you'll discover new steps on your path toward greater joy.

Exercise: Setting Your Intention

Now it's time to set your intention for this week. (For example, "My intention is to cultivate greater joy in my life.")

It's important to write down your intention as an invitation to yourself. You can record it here or in your journal.

My intention is _____

Today's Date

Take a moment to connect with your intention.

- *Take a deep breath and slowly release it.*
- *Recall a time in your life when you were filled with joy. Were you laughing, feeling a sense of playfulness, experiencing the beauty of nature, connecting with a loved one, or something else?*

As you open your heart to greater joy in the days ahead, keep this experience in mind.

Each day this week, you'll read about a new practice for cultivating joy. Try these practices one day at a time, and if one practice doesn't work for you, just repeat another practice. At the end of the week, as you look back, reflect on your experiences and choose a favorite practice to take with you on your continuing path to inner peace.

CULTIVATING HABITS OF JOY
WEEK 9, DAY 2

Many of us don't actively cultivate joy because we live in a culture that emphasizes duty and responsibility. There's work to finish, bills to pay, groceries to buy, meals to prepare, cleaning chores, laundry, and the list goes on. And we may have an inner critic that says play is for children and doing things that bring us joy is a waste of time.

Positive psychology research, however, reveals just the opposite. North Carolina psychologist Barbara Fredrickson, Ph.D., has discovered that happiness, joy, playfulness, and humor can make a positive difference in our lives. She's found that joy improves our emotional and physical health, broadens our outlook, builds our resources, and even increases our creativity (2009). And hope advocate Kathryn Goetzke (2022) recommends developing "happiness habits" as one of the five essential keys to hope.

Like eating a balanced diet, living a balanced life means making healthy choices, cultivating habits that bring us joy. We can begin by paying more attention to the good things in our lives and taking more time to appreciate them. Psychologists call this process *savoring*, which can significantly increase our positive outlook (Jose et al., 2012). Research has shown that even during troubled times, brief moments of savoring can help us cope, broaden our perspective, and help us make wiser choices (Fredrickson, 2009; Hurley & Kwon, 2013).

We can also cultivate greater joy by bringing more happy activities into our days. Sometimes, this means reaching out to follow our curiosity or reconnecting with what we loved to do as children.

Jerry Lynch, Ph.D., and author of 19 books has developed a practice he calls "Win the Day," the title of a book by the same name (Lynch, 2019). He began by listing ten activities that build energy, health, and positivity. This includes getting enough sleep, meditation, exercising, eating nutritious food, spending time in nature, reading, writing, reaching out to people who matter, avoiding toxic substances and making a difference in another's life. He keeps a list of ten things that help him live his best life by his desk, looks at them at the end of the day, and says, "If I do seven out of those ten, I win the day" (J. Lynch, personal communication, July 26, 2023).

Beginning and ending our days with positive reflection can also bring more joy into our lives. Research has shown that focusing on something to look forward to each morning can give you a boost of joy (Lickerman, 2023;

Schubert, 2012). You can wake up with the promise of new possibilities, thinking, "Today I get to....".

At the end of the day, pausing to focus on what you're grateful for can bring you a sense of wonder, joy, and renewed connection with the world. The daily gratitude practice is one of the most powerful interventions in positive psychology. Research has shown that it can increase your happiness and improve your health, relieve stress, lower your blood pressure, strengthen your immune system, and reduce the risk of depression and anxiety (Emmons, 2007; Emmons & Stern, 2013). You'll learn more about cultivating gratitude later in this chapter.

Exercise: Cultivating Habits of Joy.

This week, I invite you to cultivate some new habits of joy in your life. Think about what brings you joy:

- *a favorite hobby;*
- *exercising;*
- *getting together with friends;*
- *learning something new;*
- *listening to your favorite music; or*
- *something else?*

To cultivate greater joy in your life, you could choose to include some of these into your daily activities. Or you might consider savoring your positive experiences or coming up with a list of how you can "Win the Day."

Whatever you choose, write your experience here or in your journal.

****

Habits of Joy Practice: _____

Date

Some activities that make me happy are:

_____

I will create new happiness habits for myself by:

_____

RECONNECTING WITH YOUR BODY
WEEK 9, DAY 3

Another path to joy is mindfully reconnecting with your body. Psychologist Peter Levine, Ph.D., has found that "the full presence of mind and body" can restore our energy, enthusiasm, and joy in life (2008, p. 80).

Some of us have had a hard time developing this "full presence" with our bodies. I grew up in a military household that emphasized duty and discipline. Responding to my body's needs was often seen as laziness and self-indulgence. It's taken years for me to realize how reconnecting with my body can make me more aware of how I feel and who I am.

Today's popular stereotypes have made many of us excessively critical of our bodies. Comparing ourselves to celebrities can make us feel inferior because we don't conform to unrealistic external standards. Yet, each one of us is a unique expression of life. Today's practices will invite you to develop a kinder, more compassionate attitude towards your body.

Our bodies can reveal feelings hidden beneath the conscious surface of our awareness. Take a moment now to tune into your body. What are you feeling? Relaxed? Tense? Tired? Anxious? Hungry? Thirsty? Sleepy? Restless? Or something else?

One helpful practice is to pause for a mindful moment during the day to reconnect with your body, asking "How do I feel?" and "What do I need?" The answer might be taking a moment to rest, have a snack, get a drink of water, or if you've been sitting for a while, to get up and walk around.

We can become disconnected from our bodies when we spend too much time sitting. For centuries, our ancestors lived in hunter-gatherer or agrarian communities when regular movement supported their metabolic needs. Now we sit for hours each day driving our cars, working at our computers, watching television, and looking at our phones. Research has found that all this sitting is bad for our emotional and physical health (Sanchez-Villegas et al., 2008; Thorp et al., 2011).

Even working out for an hour at the gym three or four days a week doesn't counteract the adverse effects of excessive sitting. What *does* help is taking short breaks. This can be a simple change in your routines. Getting up to stand and walk around for even five minutes every hour or so can reduce cardiovascular risk, restore normal glucose metabolism, and help you feel happier and more vital (Dunstan et al., 2012).

Another way we can get disconnected from our bodies is by cramming too many activities into our days (Robinson & Godbey, 2005). We've gotten increased time pressure from technology, as mobile phones make us available 24/7, subject to constant interruptions. When we become too busy, rushing from one task to another produces chronic stress, which can undermine our health, happiness, and personal relationships (Easwaran, 2016).

Many practices can help us get back in touch with our bodies. One of these is the body scan, developed by Jon Kabat-Zinn as part of Mindfulness Based Stress Reduction or MBSR (2023, pp. 154-155) . Research has shown that practicing the body scan can significantly decrease reactivity and anxiety, bringing us greater peace of mind (Carmody & Baer, 2008).

You can try this simple version of the body scan now if you like.

- Take a few moments to lie down or sit comfortably in a safe place. Breathing slowly and deeply, notice how you feel as you focus on your feet, perhaps wiggling your toes with awareness.

- Then breathe awareness into your ankles and slowly move your awareness up your legs to your calves and shins, noticing how each part feels.

- Move your awareness up to your knees and calves, taking another deep mindful breath and releasing it. What do you notice? Is there tension, discomfort, relaxation, or something else?

- Now breathe awareness into your torso and your back, noticing how you feel there—Tightness? Tension? Calm? Or something else? Breathe into this area with compassionate awareness.

- Move your awareness up to your shoulders, your neck and throat, and then your head. Taking a deep mindful breath and slowly releasing it as you focus on each area, notice how it feels.

- Then move your attention down your arms, to your hands and fingers. Feel the energy in your palms as you take another mindful breath and release it.

- Now take a slow, deep breath as you feel the oneness of your whole body, filled with awareness, energy, and light.

You can also restore your connection to your body with regular exercise, which not only maintains physical health but also can raise your mood and relieve depression. The standard recommendation is to exercise 30 minutes a day five days a week or take short 10-minute exercise breaks throughout the day (Daley, 2008).

Studies have shown how walking in a wooded area or local park can relieve depression and restore your overall wellbeing (Townsend, 2006). Taking a short walk outside can also increase your creativity (Oppezzo & Schwartz, 2014). When I'm feeling blocked on a writing project, simply stepping outside for a few moments to look up at the sky can bring me an expansive sense of renewal.

Research has also shown that your posture affects your mood. Slumping and slouching can induce feelings of sadness, helplessness, and negative thoughts, while an upright posture can produce increased expansiveness, joy, and confidence (Van Cappellan, et al., 2022). I'm wondering if today's rising rates of anxiety and depression are somehow related to the hours we spend slumping over our phones and computers. Now, when I catch myself slumping, I take a deep breath and straighten my posture.

Finally, you can raise your mood by simply smiling. Because our bodies and emotions are intrinsically linked, we not only smile when we're happy, but the act of smiling can actually make us feel happier. Researchers found that when people held a pen in their mouths with their teeth horizontally, activating the muscles involved in smiling, they felt significantly happier than when they held the pen by pursing their lips (Strack, et al., 1988).

Exercise: Reconnecting with Your Body.

Today I invite you to practice at least one of these ways to reconnect with your body. Perhaps you can:

- *check in with how you're feeling during the day;*
- *adjust your posture;*
- *notice if you're rushing and slow down;*
- *take a short walk outside; or*
- *remember to smile more often.*

Whatever you choose, write your experience here or in your journal.

****

Reconnecting with Your Body Practice: _____

Date

I've chosen to reconnect with my body by:

_____

When I did this, I experienced:

_____

_____

PLAYING WITH PLAYFULNESS
WEEK 9, DAY 4

When was the last time you felt really playful—having fun, laughing, and enjoying life?

Play comes naturally to children. When I was a child, I loved playing marbles, climbing trees, and playing hide-and-go-seek and touch football with my friends. Research has found that childhood play develops our brains, especially our ability to learn, create, and build our bonds of friendship (Fredrickson, 2002; Panksepp, 1998).

What we may *not* realize is that playfulness is equally important for us as adults. We often can get so caught up in our duties and responsibilities that we forget to play. Yet, playful behavior can bring greater joy and energy to our days. Research has shown that it can expand our perspective, help relieve depression, and increase our wellbeing and joy in life (Proyer et al., 2021). Play makes us stronger and more resilient, building our personal resources and ability to flourish (Fredrickson & Joiner, 2002).

Research has also revealed the amazing power of laughter. One of the 24 character strengths common to humanity (Peterson & Seligman, 2004), a sense of humor can improve both our emotional and physical health. Research has found that laughter can raise our mood, strengthen our memory, enhance our creativity, reduce anxiety, and help us cope with stressful situations (Savage et al., 2017). Studies have also shown that laughing can relieve tension, reduce pain, and strengthen our immune system (Yim, 2016).

In the 1970s, journalist Norman Cousins experienced these effects for himself. Diagnosed with ankylosing spondylitis, a painful, incurable inflammatory disorder, he partnered with his doctor on an innovative program of positive emotions to strengthen his immune system. Watching old episodes of *Candid Camera* and Marx Brothers movies in his hospital room, he found that ten minutes of laughter had an anesthetic effect that relieved his pain and helped him sleep. He also experienced a significant drop in his blood sedimentation rate, indicating a reduction in inflammation. In a little over a week, he could move his thumbs without pain, and then he progressively regained his health. Cousins described his remarkable recovery in his book, *Anatomy of an Illness* (1979). Years later, I interviewed him at the UCLA medical school, where he'd become an adjunct professor, continuing to explore and share with others the powerful connection between positive emotions and health.

As we deal with our challenging world today, developing greater playfulness can bring us hope on many levels. Exiled from his home in Tibet, the Dalai Lama has faced many challenges. Yet now he works with neuroscientists conducting research on the effects of meditation on our brains and also works for world peace. Whenever I think of him, I recall his infectious laughter, playfulness, and the joy he experiences in the present moment.

There are many ways that you, too, can add greater playfulness to your days. What is playful varies for different people. I enjoy playing the piano, growing vegetables in my garden, playing with my dog, and sharing laughter with my friends, who have their own playful pursuits. Simone plays pick-up basketball with colleagues on campus. Tracey hikes in the woods, Carol paints landscapes, and Will has fun cooking special meals for his friends.

EXERCISE: Playing with Playfulness.

How can you experience greater playfulness? I invite you to discover one new way to reconnect with the spirit of play. Perhaps you can:

- *spend time with a hobby you enjoy;*
- *watch a comedy show;*
- *play a game with friends; or*
- *do something else you enjoy.*

Whatever you choose, write your experience here or in your journal.

****

My Playing with Playfulness Practice: _____

Date

I've chosen this way to experiment with playfulness:

_____

When I did this, I experienced:

_____

THE JOY OF GIVING
WEEK 9, DAY 5

Reaching out to others can make us feel better, relieve our stress, improve our emotional and physical health, and bring us greater purpose, joy, and well-being Preventive medicine doctor Stephen Post, MD, has found that we can improve our health when we "step back from self-preoccupation and self-worry" and that the best way to do this is by reaching out to help others (2011, p. 825).

According to Dr. Post, we can reach out in many ways—in personal relationships, community groups, and volunteer work. The key is to reach out willingly, not out of a sense of obligation, to follow our hearts, not external demands and "shoulds." As long as we balance our own needs with those of others, we'll avoid burnout and experience greater joy and meaning (Childre, 2016; Post, 2011).

Reaching out to others is important in every stage of life. Often, people feel disconnected when they retire. Without their daily work routine, they can lose their sense of connection, capability, and community. Yet, research has shown that retired people who volunteer at least 100 hours a year are healthier and have lower levels of depression, longer lives, and greater overall wellbeing (Post, 2011).

What makes giving to others so rewarding? Giving can bring feelings of joy and satisfaction as well as the euphoria, energy, and enthusiasm known as "helper's high" (Luks, 1991). These positive emotions can relieve stress, improve our mood, reduce inflammation, and strengthen our immune systems, providing us with greater joy, meaning, and confidence (Fredrickson et al., 2013; Inagaki et al., 2016; Post, 2011).

But beyond all this, reaching out to others can free us from the fear that often lurks beneath the surface of our awareness, a fear of loneliness, isolation, and helplessness. According to Buddhist scholar Thupten Jinpa, Ph.D., (2015, p. 51) when we face challenges, we can become trapped in a sense of isolation and fear. Connecting to others in regular acts of compassion and kindness can liberate us from that fear, replacing it with a sense of capability, connection, and hope.

Former United States Surgeon General Vivek Murthy, MD, has linked our current epidemic of loneliness and isolation with fear. In a world he sees as "locked in a struggle between love and fear," he urges us to reach out to others to bring hope and healing to ourselves and our world (2020, p. 280).

There are many ways to reach out to others. I've been giving talks on hope to local groups from college students to retirement communities. And since research has shown that building hope involves positive action (Feldman & Dreher, 2012; Goetzke, 2022), I've been channeling the energy I could spend worrying about politics into action. Every week, I meet on Zoom with a group of friendly volunteers who call people on Arizona Native American sovereign lands, asking how they're doing and putting them in touch with local organizers if they need anything from firewood and water to medical assistance. We also help them get their family members and communities registered to vote.

How can you reach out in compassionate connection to those around you? There are many possibilities. My friend Peter volunteers at a local animal shelter, Mary works with her church youth group, Jeannie volunteers at the local library, Steve delivers food to hungry families, and Jim hosts a weekly meditation group.

Exercise: The Joy of Giving.

How can you experience more of the joy of giving? Can you:

Reach out to help a neighbor?

Volunteer in your local community?

Join a political action group?

Or something else?

Whatever you choose, write down your experience here or in your journal.

****

My Joy of Giving Practice: _____

                                                  Date

I've chosen this way to reach out to others:

_____

When I did this, I experienced:

_____

THE LIGHT OF APPRECIATION
WEEK 9, DAY 6

My father grew up on a Kentucky farm but found his dream in the skies. As an Air Force pilot, he flew cargo planes, air rescue helicopters, and jets, and when he retired, he became a flight instructor. My favorite times were when he'd take me up in his Cessna 172 to explore the skies together, soaring over the Southern California coast and the sparkling blue Pacific Ocean.

One morning, I looked up at the gray stratus clouds overhead and thought our flight would be cancelled. But my father assured me that we could still fly that day. We headed out to the airport and took off. When the plane broke through the cloud layer, the sky was suddenly clear and blue. My father smiled. "The sun is always there," he said. "Sometimes, when we're too close to the ground, we can't see it."

We can forget that the sun is still there in our lives when our vision is clouded by stress, negative news, or everyday routines. Today, we'll explore ways to break through the clouds and look to the light. We can do this with the power of appreciation.

Appreciation helps us focus on the moments of beauty around us that we often take for granted. Psychological research has found that the appreciation of beauty and excellence is one of the 24 character strengths common to all humanity (Peterson & Seligman, 2004).

Psychologist Dan Baker, Ph.D., considers appreciation the "fundamental happiness tool" and says that when we become more aware of the beauty in our lives, we can transcend our normal world and enter "a state of grace" (Baker & Stauth, 2003, p. 81). When we open our hearts in appreciation, we can feel greater joy, meaning, and connection with life.

Appreciation brings us a sense of wonder, which Rabbi Abraham Joshua Heschel (2011, p. 51) found is too often lacking in daily life. Psychologist Barbara Fredrickson, Ph.D., (2009) encourages us to slow down, open our hearts, and breathe in the goodness around us. And as research has found, appreciation can help relieve stress, reduce inflammation, strengthen our emotional balance, and build greater hope (Adler & Fagley, 2005; Childre & Martin, 1999; Diessner et al., 2008; Stellar et al., 2015).

Appreciation can lead to awe, a deep emotional experience and spiritual connection to a greater reality beyond ourselves. We can feel awe in response to a radiant sunset, the courage or kindness of others, a beautiful symphony, or the mystery of life itself. Psychologist Dacher Keltner, Ph.D., (2023) has found that awe can bring us feelings of deep, transcendent joy and inspire us to become more curious, creative, and open to the wonders of life.

We can bring greater appreciation into our lives by building our awareness. In his research, psychologist Rhett Diessner, Ph.D., found that students develop greater hope when they write weekly descriptions of three forms of beauty they encounter—natural beauty, artistic beauty, and the moral beauty of reaching out to help others (Diessner et al., 2006; Diessner at al., 2008).

In creative writing classes, students have to write weekly essays about *something*. To bring greater hope to my students, I asked them to write short descriptions of natural, artistic, and moral beauty, and then share them with the class at the end of the week. At first, my students said it was easier to come up with examples of natural and artistic beauty than moral beauty. "What if we can't find an example of moral beauty?" one student asked. Another student responded, "Then do something helpful yourself and write about it." I smiled in appreciation, realizing how we were all learning together.

A major form of appreciation is gratitude. Psychologist Robert Emmons, Ph.D., defines gratitude as acknowledging and feeling thankful for the goodness in our lives. His research (2007; Emmons & Stern, 2013) has found that grateful people are healthier and happier, better able to cope with stress, more optimistic, resilient, and connected to others.

Research has found that the more gratitude we feel, the less we experience loneliness and isolation (Hittner & Widholm, 2024). Studies have shown that we can overcome recurrent memories of painful events by developing gratitude for what we learned, how we developed greater character, or how we perceived deeper meaning in life (Watkins et al., 2008).

Gratitude can not only increase our personal wellbeing but also strengthen our friendships and renew our communities as well (Emmons & McCullough, 2003; Fredrickson, 2004). Gratitude can also increase our spiritual wellbeing. Counting our blessings can help us appreciate the good in our lives, build our trust in a loving creator, and restore our faith in life (Watkins et al., 2024).

Exercise: The Light of Appreciation

Now it's your turn. How can you bring more of the light of appreciation into your life?

- *You can bring greater appreciation into your life by beginning a regular gratitude practice. Robert Emmons (2007) recommends pausing at the end of the day to write down three things you're grateful for.*

- *You can also practice gratitude by finding ways to thank people more often—in personal comments and thank you notes. And you can practice the tradition of saying grace before meals, giving thanks to all those who helped grow, harvest, and prepare your food, and to the source of life itself.*

- *You can begin each day with appreciation. When you wake up, you can pause to give thanks for the gifts of the day. One morning, after weeks of rain, I looked out my window. The sunlight sparkling through the raindrops on the trees like so many shimmering crystals gave me a vision of light to begin my day.*

Whatever form of appreciation you choose, write down your experience here or in your journal.

****

My Light of Appreciation Practice: _____

                                                            Date

I've chosen this appreciation practice:

_____

When I practiced this, I experienced:

_____

REFLECT AND REVIEW
WEEK 9, DAY 7

This week, you were invited to try these practices:

1. Habits of Joy

2. Reconnecting with Your Body

3. Playing with Playfulness

4. The Joy of Giving

5. The Light of Appreciation

As you look back on your week, reflect on your responses. Review how each practice made you feel, and choose at least one practice you'd like to take along on your journey to greater peace of mind. Then, write down your experience here or in your journal.

****

Week 9 Review: _____

Date

What practice would you like to take with you?

_____

What feelings does this practice inspire for you?

_____

_____

How can you use this practice to develop greater peace of mind in the days to come?

_____

CHAPTER 10

Commencement

Congratulations on completing your journey through *Pathways to Inner Peace*.

In my years as a college professor, I attended many graduations, which are also called commencements, times of celebration and new beginnings. You, too, have reached a commencement, a time to celebrate *your* accomplishments and the beginning of a new chapter in your life.

During the past weeks, you've been exploring nine powerful pathways to bring you greater connection and peace of mind:

- Mindful Presence
- Nature
- Community
- Meditation
- Kindness
- Purpose
- Intuition and Inspiration
- The Arts
- Joy

Today's busy, noisy, challenging world can often fragment our attention, undermine confidence, and leave us feeling disconnected, anxious, and confused. Yet now you've learned from research and your own experience how these nine pathways can light your way to a deeper state of connection and inner peace.

On your journey through this book, you've discovered your own favorite practices. Now it's time to make them a regular part of your life.

Repeated practice can improve our performance when we begin anything new from starting an exercise routine, to learning a new language, or playing a musical instrument. As we begin learning a new skill, neuroscience research has found that our brains start forming new neural connections (Bassett et al., 2011). Each time we practice that skill, our brains continue to grow these connections. This is why repeating your favorite practices and incorporating them into your life can transform your inner world, progressively inspiring greater peace of mind, resilience, and hope.

There are many ways you can add your favorite practices to your life:

- You can use the reinforcing power of structure, adding a favorite practice to something that you already do. For example, I start my days with coffee and meditation. The first sip of my coffee invites me to begin my morning meditation.

- You can create helpful reminders for yourself. One friend puts a note on her mirror as a reminder to savor the beauty of each day. Some of my clients wear a rubber band or special bracelet on their wrists to remind them to pause for moments of mindfulness throughout their busy days.

- You can take a few moments in the evening to reflect on what you did that day, what you learned, and what you're grateful for. This brief check-in can bring you greater understanding. And practicing gratitude can bring you greater peace of mind and build your trust in life (Emmons, 2013).

Learning is an essential part of being human. Birds can fly, fish can swim, and antelopes can run faster than we can. Our greatest strength as humans is our ability to learn, which shapes who we can become.

"The love of learning is the guide of life" (*Philosophia Bio Kybernetes*) is the motto of Phi Beta Kappa. To live with this love of learning is what psychologist Carol Dweck, Ph.D., (2006) calls a "growth mindset," the ability to learn from our efforts, and even our mistakes, so that we can progressively become wiser, more present, more creative, and more successful in life.

Neuroscience research has now shown that our brains can continue to grow throughout our lives as we continue to learn (DeMarin et al., 2014), and Dweck's research (2006) has shown that people with a growth mindset experience greater wellbeing and joy in life.

As you move forward with a growth mindset, continuing to learn and following your inner guidance, your opportunities will expand. One discovery can lead to another, revealing new possibilities, and new forms of connection. This happened to me years ago when I followed a long-deferred dream.

I rediscovered this dream while writing my book, *Your Personal Renaissance,* (2008). In my research, I learned how Renaissance artists discovered their creative gifts in childhood by reaching out with joy and curiosity to follow their hearts, to do what they loved to do. Then, I began to reflect on what I could learn from my own childhood.

As a child, I used to enjoy visiting my grandmother in Pasadena, California, who loved music and Shakespeare, and found joy in everything around her. She'd often sweep me up in a warm, fragrant hug, and take me to her kitchen where I'd help her snap green beans and watch her make her wonderful apple and cherry pies.

One day, when I reached up to touch the keys of her baby grand piano, she asked, "Sweetheart, do you want to play the piano?" I nodded—"yes." So, she spoke to my mother, offering to get me lessons and even to give me her piano. But no. My mother said that because we moved so often for my father's Air Force assignments, having a piano was out of the question.

As the years went by, we moved from California to the Philippine Islands and then to Grandview, Missouri, where I made a new friend, Bonnie Bennett, who lived down the street. Bonnie's father was also in the Air Force, and she played the piano, a blond spinet in their living room. Bonnie taught me some chords, and I had lots of fun as we played a few simple songs together.

My dad must have noticed how much I loved playing Bonnie's piano because one day—I could hardly believe it—he came home with a blue Air Force pickup truck, two young airmen in the cab, and a piano in the back. I jumped up and down in excitement when the young men unloaded the piano. It was an old black upright, and the ivory on some of the keys was gone. My mother told them to put it in the basement because she didn't want it in her living room.

A basement is not the best place for a piano because the dampness can make it go out of tune, but it became my musical sanctuary. I began taking lessons from Bonnie's piano teacher, and for the next year, every day after school, I'd go down to the basement to practice chords, learn new songs, and play some simplified classical pieces. The music filled my mind and body, taking me into a new reality. I was just a shy, skinny kid with pigtails, but playing the piano connected me to something larger than myself—beautiful, inspirational, and strong.

The next year when my father was transferred to a radar site in Nebraska, I had to say goodbye to Bonnie, and my mother insisted that we leave the piano, my dear piano, behind. When I was in high school, I got myself a guitar and began playing folk songs, but it was never quite the same.

Looking back years later, I realized that I still missed playing the piano. With Bob's encouragement, I went to a music store, bought an introductory piano book, and rented an electronic keyboard. I found I could still play chords and began playing simple songs. But to make any progress, I needed lessons.

When we reach out for new possibilities, we can often experience synchronicities. One Sunday, I saw an ad in the church bulletin from a local piano teacher named Veronica. I called her and signed up for my first lesson which led to many more. More music, more lessons, more joy and discoveries. I loved playing Veronica's Chickering grand piano during my lessons. Then, I'd go home to practice on the keyboard. It has sounded good at first, but its plastic keys had no resonance, no soul. It felt like playing a computer.

I searched the web and local piano stores, but the pianos were all so expensive. Then one day, I got a call from Randy, Veronica's piano tuner, who said he'd seen a used piano with a low price because its finish was worn and faded. So, I drove to a nearby town where a salesman took me into a warehouse where I saw this long-neglected piano. Its finish was faded, and it had water stains from flower pots that had been placed on its lid. Some of its ivory keys were chipped. But when I sat down on the bench and touched its keys, my eyes filled with tears. It had a beautiful resonant sound that echoed back to another time. It was a 1938 Steinway baby grand that began making music when Franklin Roosevelt was president.

After months of refinishing, my piano now stands in our living room, its beautiful walnut finish reminding me of my grandmother's piano so long ago. And whenever I play it, I feel connected—to the music, my grandmother, and the long history that brought this piano into my life. And as one connection often leads to another, my piano teacher, Veronica, has become like a sister to me, filling my life with grace notes on many levels.

New harmonies can also come to you as you follow your favorite practices and listen to your inner guidance. You, too, may find that one connection can lead to another, expanding your sense of possibility and bringing greater joy into your life.

And if you ever feel disconnected, lost in the shadows of worry and self-doubt, the practices in this book can help you reconnect, becoming a guide to discovering greater harmony and renewal. You can reread a favorite pathway or open the book at random to discover a practice that renews your hope on your continuing journey to inner peace.

I'd love to hear how these pathways work for you. You can contact me at https://www.dianedreher.com.

I wish you joy on your life's journey.

Diane

References

Adler, M. G., & Fagley, N.S. (2005). Appreciation: Individual differences in finding value and meaning as a unique predictor of subjective well-being. *Journal of Personality, 73* (1), 79-113.

Aftab, A. (2020). Meaning in life and its relationship with physical, mental, and cognitive functioning: A study of 1,042 community-dwelling adults across the lifespan. *Journal of Clinical Psychiatry, 81* (1), 19m13064.

Alcock, I., White, M. P., Wheeler, B. W., Fleming, L. E., & Depledge, M. H. (2014). Longitudinal effects on mental health of moving to greener and less green urban areas. *Environmental Science & Technology, 48,* 1247-1255.

Alcoholics Anonymous. *Alcoholics Anonymous.* (1976) Third Edition. New York, NY: Alcoholics Anonymous World Services, Inc.

Alfrey, A., Field, V., Xenophontes, I., & Holttum, S. (2021). Identifying the mechanisms of poetry therapy and associated effects on participants: A synthesized review of empirical literature. *The Arts in Psychotherapy, 75,* 101832. https://www.sciencedirect.com/science/article/abs/pii/S0197455621000770?via%3Dihub

Algoe, S. B., & Haidt, J. (2009). Witnessing excellence in action: The 'other-praising' emotions of elevation, gratitude, and admiration. *The Journal of Positive Psychology, 4,* 105-127.

Antonovsky, A. (1980). *Health, stress, and coping.* San Francisco, CA: Jossey-Bass.

Assagioli, R. (1973). *The act of will.* Baltimore, MD: Penguin Books.

Assagioli, R. (1976). *Psychosynthesis.* New York, NY: Viking Press.

Atchley, R. A., Strayer, D. L., & Atchley, P. (2012). Creativity in the wild: Improving creative reasoning through immersion in natural settings. *PLosONE 7* (12): e1474.doi:101371/journal.pone.0051474.

Baker, D. & Stauth, C. (2003). *What happy people know.* Kutztown, PA: Rodale Press.

Balban, M. Y., Neri, E., Kogon, M. M., Zeitzer, J. M., & Huberman, A. D. (2023, January 17). Brief structured respiration practices enhance mood and reduce physiological arousal. *Cell Reports Medicine, 4,* 100895.

Bartsch, A. (2012). Emotional gratification in entertainment experience: Why viewers of movies and television series find it rewarding to experience emotions. *Media Psychology, 15* (3), 267-302.

Bassett, D. S., Wymbs, N. F., Porter, M. A., Mucha, P. J., Carlson, J. M., & Grafton, S. T. (2011). Dynamic reconfiguration of human brain networks during learning. *Proceedings of the National Academy of Sciences, 108*(18), 7641-7646.

Beauregard, M., & O'Leary, D. (2007). *The spiritual brain: A neuroscientist's case for the existence of the soul.* New York, NY: HarperCollins.

Beck, R. J., Cesario, T. C., Yousefi, A., & Enamoto, H. (2000). Choral singing, performance perception, and immune system changes in salivary immunoglobulin A and cortisol. *Music Perception, 18,* 87-106.

Berman, M.G., Kross, E., Krpan, K.M., Askren, M. K., Burson, A., Deldin, P. J., Kaplan, S., Sherdell, L., Gotlip, I. H., Jonides, J. (2012). Interacting with nature improves cognition and affect for individuals with depression. *Journal of Affective Disorders, 140,* 300-305.

Berns-Zare, I. & Hayman, T. (2022). Naso: Awakening to God's protection and presence, in Strassfeld, M. (Ed.) *Torah without end,* 70-71. Teaneck, N.J.: Ben Yehuda Press.

Berrios, R., Totterdell, P., & Kellett, S. (2018). When feeling mixed can be meaningful: The relation between mixed emotions and eudaimonic well-being. *Journal of Happiness Studies, 19,* 841-861.

Billings, L. (2022, October 2). Explorers of quantum entanglement win 2022 Nobel Prize in Physics. *Scientific American.* https://www.scientificamerican.com/article/explorers-of-quantum-entanglement-win-2022-nobel-prize-in-physics1/

Blake, W. (1863). From "Auguries of Innocence," lines 1-4. First published by Alexander Gilchrist and Dante Gabriel Rossetti (1863) in *Life of William Blake Pictor Ignotus with selections from his poems and other writings,* London, UK: Macmillan. In D. V. Erdman & H. Bloom (Eds.). (1982). *The complete poetry and prose of William Blake.* Berkeley and Los Angeles, CA: University of California press.

Block, E. P., Wong, M.D., Kataoka, S. H., & Zimmerman, F. J. (2022). A symphony within: Frequent participation in performing arts predicts higher positive mental health in young adults. *Social Science & Medicine, 292,* 114615.

Boorstein, S. (2002). *Pay attention, for goodness sake.* New York, NY: Ballentine Books.

Bormann, J. E. (2010). Mantram repetition: A "portable contemplative practice" for modern times. In T. G. Plante (Ed.), *Contemplative practices in action* (pp. 78-99). Santa Barbara, CA: Praeger.

Bormann, J. E., Hurst, S., & Kelly, A. (2013). Responses to mantram repetition program from veterans with posttraumatic stress disorder: A qualitative analysis. *JRRD, 50,* 769-784.

Boss, P. (2022). *The myth of closure: Ambiguous loss in a time of pandemic and change.* New York, NY: W.W. Norton & Company.

Bowlby, J. (1969). *Attachment and loss* (Vol. I: Attachment). New York, NY: Basic Books.

Bowlby, J. (1973). *Attachment and loss* (Vol. 2: Separation.) New York, NY: Basic Books.

Bowlby, J. (1980). *Attachment and loss* (Vol. 3: Loss, sadness and depression). New York, NY: Basic Books.

Brandling, J., & House, W. (2009). Social prescribing in general practice: Adding meaning to medicine. *British Journal of General Practice, 59* (563), 454-456.

Bratman, G. N., Hamilton, J. P., & Daily, G.C. (2012). The impacts of nature experience on human cognitive function and mental health. *Annals of the New York Academy of Sciences, 1249,* 118-136.

Brooks, David. (2023). *How to know a person: The art of seeing others deeply and being deeply seen.* New York, NY: Random House.

Brooks, H.L., Rushton, K., Lovell, K., Bee, P., Walker, L., Grant, L., & Rogers, A. (2018). The power of support from companion animals for people living with mental health problems: A systematic review and narrative synthesis of the evidence. *BMC Psychiatry, 18* (31), doi 10.1186/s12888-018-1613-2

Buber, M. (1956). "I and thou" in W. Herberg (Ed.). *The writings of Martin Buber,* pp. 43-62. New York, NY: Meridian Books.

Carmody, J., & Baer, R. A. (2008). Relationships between mindfulness practice and levels of mindfulness, medical and psychological symptoms and well-being in a mindfulness-based stress reduction program. *Journal of Behavioral Medicine, 31*(1), 23–33.

Challenge Success. (2024). Stanford, CA: Stanford University. https://challengesuccess.org

Chandra, M. L., & Levitin, D.J. (2013). The neurochemistry of music. *Trends in Cognitive Sciences, 17* (4), 179-193.

Charnetski, C. J., Riggers, S., & Brennan, F. X. (2004). Effect of petting a dog on immune system function. *Psychological Reports, 95*(3 suppl), 1087-1091.

Childre, D. (2016) Care vs overcare. Compassion: The need of the times. In D. Childre, H. Martin, D. Rozman, & R. McCraty, (Eds.) (2016). *Heart intelligence: Connecting with the intuitive wisdom of the heart,* (pp. 213-240). Lumsden, SK, Canada: Waterfront Press.

Childre, D. & Martin, H. with Beech, D. (1999). *The HeartMath solution.* New York, NY: HarperCollins.

Childre, D., Martin, H., Rozman, D., & McCraty, R. (2016). *Heart intelligence: Connecting with the intuitive wisdom of the heart.* Lumsden, SK, Canada: Waterfront Press.

Childre, D., & Rozman, D. (2005). *Transforming stress: The HeartMath solution for relieving worry, fatigue, and tension.* Oakland, CA: New Harbinger Publications.

Cho, L.Y., Miller, J., Hrastar, M.., Sutton, N.A., & Younes, J.P. (2009, December). Synchronicity awareness intervention: An open trial. *Teachers College Record, 111*(12), 2786-2799.

Cohen, G. L. (2022). *Belonging: The science of creating connection and bridging divides.* New York, NY: W. W. Norton & Company.

Collins, H. K., Hagerty, S. F., Quoidbach, J., Norton, M. I., & Brooks, A. W. (2022). Relational diversity in social portfolios predicts well-being. *PNAS, 119* (43), 1-9.

Cousins, N. (1979). *Anatomy of an illness as perceived by the patient.* New York, NY: W.W. Norton & Company.

Cregg, D.R., & Cheavens, J. S.(2022). Healing through helping: An experimental investigation of kindness, social activities, and reappraisal as well-being interventions. *The Journal of Positive Psychology, 18* (6), 924-941.

Creswell, J.D., Irwi, M.R., Burklund, L.J., Lieberman, M.D., Arevalo, J.M.G., Ma, J. et al. (2012). Mindfulness-Based Stress Reduction training reduces loneliness and pro-inflammatory gene expression in older adults: A small randomized controlled trial. *Brain, Behavior, and Immunity, 26,* 1095-1101.

Csikszentmihalyi, M. (1990). *Flow: The psychology of optimal experience.* New York. NY: HarperCollins

Csikszentmihalyi, M. (1997). *Finding flow.* New York, NY: HarperCollins.

Dalai Lama. (1995). *The power of compassion: A collection of lectures By His Holiness the XIV Dalai Lama* (trans. G. T. Jinpa). San Francisco, CA: Thorsons.

Daley, A. (2008). Exercise and depression: A review of reviews. *Journal of Clinical Psychology in Medical Settings, 15,* 140-147.

Daltry, R.M., & Mehr, K. E. (2015). Therapy dogs on campus: Recommendations for counseling center outreach, *Journal of College Student Psychotherapy, 29,* 72-78;

Dante Alighieri. (1921). *The Divine Comedy of Dante Alighieri. The Italian text with a translation in English blank verse and a commentary by Courtney Langdon, Vol. 3 Paradiso.* Cambridge, MA: Harvard University

Press, 1921, p. 394. Originally published c. 1321. My translation of the last line of Dante's *Paradiso,* line 145, *L'Amor che mouve il sole e l'altre stele.*

Dante Alighieri. (1955). *La divina commedia.* N. Sapegno (Ed.). Vol. 1. *Inferno,* p. 1. Firenze, IT: La Nuova Italia Editrice. Originally published c. 1321. My translation of the first two lines of Dante's *Divine Comedy, Nel mezzo del cammin di nostra vita mi ritrovai per una selva oscura.*

Darley, J. M., & Batson, C. D. (1973). "From Jerusalem to Jericho:" A study of situation and dispositional variables in helping behavior. *Journal of Personality and Social Psychology, 27,* 100-108.

Delbecq, A. L. (2010). How spirituality is manifested within corporate culture: Perspectives from a case study and a scholar's focus group. *Journal of Management, Spirituality & Religion, 7,* 51-71.

De Leeuw, R.N. H., Jaicke-Bowles, S.H., & Ji, Q. (2021). How music awakens the heart: An experimental study on music, emotions, and connectedness. *Mass Communication and Society,* doi: 10.1080/15205436.2021.1956542.

DeMarin, V., Morovic, S., & Béné, R. (2014). Neuroplasticity. *Periodicum Biologorum, 116* (2), 209-211.

Després, C. (1991, Summer). The meaning of home: Literature review and directions for future research and theoretical development. *Journal of Architectural and Planning Research, 8* (2), 96-115.

Dienstman, A. M. (2019, Oct 14). One mayor transformed his town in the city of kindness. *Goodnet: Gateway to doing good. https://www.goodnet. org/articles/one-mayor-transformed-his-town-into-city-kindness.*

Diessner, R., Rust, T. Solom, R. C., Frost, N. & Parsons, L. (2006). Beauty and hope: A moral beauty intervention. *Journal of Moral Education, 35,* 301-317.

Diessner, R., Solom, R. C., Frost, N. K., & Parsons, L. (2008). Engagement with beauty: Appreciating natural, artistic, and moral beauty. *Journal of Personality, 142* (3), 303-329.

Dijksterhuis, A., Bos, M. W., Nordgren, L.F., & van Baaren, R.B.(2006, February 17). On making the right choice: The Deliberation-Without-Attention Effect. *Science, 311,* 1005-1007.

Dijksterhuis, A., & Nordgren, L. (2006). A theory of unconscious thought. *Perspectives on Psychological Science, 1,* 95-109.

Diliberto-Macaluso, K. A., & Stubblefield, B. L. (2015). The use of painting for short-term mood and arousal improvement. *Psychology of Aesthetics, Creativity, and the Arts, 9,* 228-234.

Djikic, M., Oatley, K., & Moldoveanu, M. C.(2013). Reading other minds: Effects of literature on empathy. *Scientific Study of Literature, 3*(1), 28-47.

Donne, J. (1965). *Devotions upon emergent occasions.* Ann Arbor, MI: University of Michigan Press. Originally published 1624.

Dossey, L. (2013). *One mind: How our individual mind is part of a greater consciousness and why it matters.* Carlsbad, CA: Hay House.

Doty, J. R. (2016). *Into the magic shop: A neurosurgeon's quest to discover the mysteries of the brain and the secrets of the heart.* New York, NY: Penguin Random House.

Dreher, D. E. (1998). *The Tao of womanhood.* New York, NY: William Morrow.

Dreher, D. E. (2000). *The Tao of inner peace.* New York, NY: Penguin Putnam.

Dreher, D.E. (2001). *Inner gardening: Four seasons of cultivating the soil and spirit.* New York: HarperCollins, 2001.

Dreher, D. E. (2008). *Your personal Renaissance: 12 steps to finding your life's true calling.* Cambridge, MA: DaCapo Press.

Dreher, D. E. (2015). Leading with compassion: A moral compass for our time. In T. G. Plante (Ed.). *The psychology of compassion and cruelty: Understanding the emotional, spiritual, and religious influences* (pp.73-87). Santa Barbara, CA: ABC-CLIO.

Dreher, D. E. (2022, October 7). Turning from depression to the light of hope. Your personal renaissance. PsychologyToday.com https://www.psychologytoday.com/intl/blog/your-personal-renaissance/202210/turning-depression-the-light-hope._

Dreher, D. E. (2023, December 4). How can you deal with stress and lack of control? Five steps for dealing with ambiguous loss. *Psychologytoday.com.* https://www.psychologytoday.com/intl/blog/your-personal-renaissance/202312/how-can-you-deal-with-stress-and-lack-of-control.

Dunstan, D. W., Kingwell, B. A., Larsen, R., Healy, G. N., Cerin, E., Hamilton, M. T., Shaw, J. E., Bertovic, D. A., Zimmet, P. Z., Salmon, J., & Owen, N. (2012). Breaking up prolonged sitting reduces postprandial glucose and insulin responses. *Diabetes Care, 35,* 976-983.

Dutton, J. E., & Heaphy, E. D. (2003). The power of high-quality connections. In K.S. Cameron, J. E. Dutton, & R. E. Quinn (Eds.). *Positive organizational scholarship* (pp. 263-278). San Francisco, CA: Berrett-Koehler Publishers.

Dweck, C. S. (2006). *Mindset: The new psychology of success.* New York, NY: Random House.

Easwaran. E. (2001). *The constant companion.* Tomales, CA: Nilgiri Press.

Easwaran, E. (2016). *Passage meditation: A complete spiritual practice.* Tomales, CA: Nilgiri Press.

Easwaran, E. (2008). *The mantram handbook: A practical guide for choosing your mantram & calming your mind.* Tomales, CA: Nilgiri Press. See also the Blue Mountain Center of Meditation website at https://www.bmcm.org/learn/mantram/.

Einstein, A. (1950). In A. Calaprice (Ed.), *The new quotable Einstein.* Princeton, NJ: Princeton University Press.

Ellis, L. (2021; 2025 rev). *Essence of an artist: Follow your dream.* For more information, see www.LorenEllisArt.com.

Emerson, R. W. (1903). *Nature: Addresses and lectures.* Boston, MA: Houghton Mifflin.

Emerson, R. W. (1926). Art. In *Essays by Ralph Waldo Emerson.* E. Edman (Introd.), pp. 246-259. New York, NY: Thomas Y. Crowell Company.

Emmons, R. A. (2007). *Thanks! How practicing gratitude can make you happier.* Boston, MA: Houghton Mifflin.

Emmons, R. A. (2013). *Gratitude works!: A twenty-one-day program for creating emotional prosperity.* San Francisco, CA: Jossey-Bass.

Emmons, R.A. & McCullough, M. E. (2003). Counting blessings versus burdens: An experimental investigation of gratitude and subjective well-being in daily life. *Journal of Personality and Social Psychology, 84* (2), 377-389.

Emmons, R. A., & Stern, R. (2013). Gratitude as a therapeutic intervention. *Journal of Clinical Psychology, 69* (8), 846-855.

Farley, K. M. J., & Veitch, J. A. (2001, August 15). A room with a view: A review of the effects of windows on work and well-being. *Institute for Research in Construction.* IRC research report RR 136.

Feldman, D. B., and Dreher, D. E. (2012). Can hope be changed in 90 minutes? Testing the efficacy of a single-session goal-pursuit intervention for college students. *Journal of Happiness Studies, 13,* 745-759.

Feldman, D.B., & Kravitz, L. D. (2014). *Supersurvivors: The surprising link between suffering and success.* New York, NY: HarperCollins.

Ferguson, J. K. (2010). Centering prayer: A method of Christian meditation for our time. In T. G. Plante (Ed.).*Contemplative practices in action* (pp.60-77). Santa Barbara, CA: Praeger.

Field, W. & Kruger, C. (2008). The effects of art psychotherapy intervention on levels of depression and health locus of control orientations experienced by black women living with HIV. *South African Journal of Psychology, 38,* 467-478.

Foerde, K., Knowlton, B. J., & Poldrack, R. A. (2006). Modulation of competing memory systems by distraction. *Proceedings of the National Academy of Sciences, 103,* 11778-11783.

Fontaine, D.K., Briggs, L. P., Pope-Smith, B. (2001). Designing humanistic critical care environments. *Critical Care Nursing Quarterly,* 24 (3), 21-34.

Frankl, V.E. (1984). *Man's search for meaning.* New York, NY: Washington Square Press. Originally published in 1959.

Fredrickson, B. L. (2001). The role of positive emotions in positive psychology. *American Psychologist, 56,* 218-226.

Fredrickson, B. L. (2002). Positive emotions. In C. R. Snyder & S. J. Lopez (Eds.). *Handbook of positive psychology,* (pp. 120-134). New York, NY: Oxford University Press.

Fredrickson, B. L. (2003). The value of positive emotions. *The American Scientist, 91,* 330-335.

Fredrickson, B.L. (2004). Gratitude, like other positive emotions, broadens and builds. R.A. Emmons & M. E. McCullough (Eds.). *The psychology of gratitude* (pp. 145-165). New York, NY: Oxford University Press.

Fredrickson, B.L. (2009). *Positivity: Discover the upward spiral that will change your life*. New York, NY: Harmony Books.

Fredrickson, B. L. (2013). *Love 2.0: How our supreme emotion affects everything we feel, think, do, and become*. New York, NY: Hudson Street Press.

Fredrickson, B. L., Cohn, M. A., Coffey, K. A., Pek, J., & Finkel, S. M. (2008). Open hearts build lives: Positive emotions, induced through loving-kindness meditation, build consequential personal resources. *Journal of Personality and Social Psychology, 95*, 1045-1062.

Fredrickson, B. L., Grewen, K. M., Coffey, K. A., Algoe, S. A., Firestine, A. M., Arevalo, J. M. G. , Ma, J., & Cole, S. W. (2013, August). A functional genomic perspective on human well-being. *PNAS, 110* (33), 13684-13689.

Fredrickson, B. & Joiner, T. (2002). Positive emotions trigger upward spirals toward emotional well-being. *Psychological Science, 13*, 172-175.

Frost, R. (2024). "The Road Not Taken." *Mountain interval*. Alpha edition. Originally published 1916.

Frydman, J. S. (2016). Role theory and executive function: Constructing cooperative paradigms of drama therapy and cognitive neuropsychology. *The Arts in Psychotherapy, 47*, 41-47.

Garland, E.L. (2007). The meaning of mindfulness: A second-order cybernetics of stress, metacognition, and coping. *Complementary Health Practice Review, 12* (1), 15-30.

Garland, E. L., Fredrickson, B., Kring, A. M., Johnson, D. P., Meyer, P. S., & Penn, D. L. (2010). Upward spirals of positive emotions counter downward spirals of negativity: Insights from the broaden-and-build theory and affective neuroscience on the treatment of emotion dysfunctions and deficits in psychopathology. *Clinical Psychology Review, 30*, 849-864.

George, L. K., Ellison, C. G., & Larson, D. B. (2002). Explaining the relationships between religious involvement and health. *Psychological Inquiry, 13* (3), 190-200.

Goetzke, K. (2022). *The biggest little book about hope*. (2nd edition). New York, NY: Morgan James Publishing.

Goleman, D., & Davidson, R.J. (2017). *Altered traits: How meditation changes your mind, brain, and body*. New York, NY: Penguin Random House.

Graham, C.(2023). *The power of hope: How the science of well-being can save us from despair*. Princeton, NJ: Princeton University Press.

Habibi, A., Damasio, H., & Damasio, A. (2021). Music education and child development. In M. Beckerman & P. Boghossian (Eds). *Classical music* (pp. 29-37). Cambridge, UK: Open Book Publishers.

Haidt, J. (2000). The positive emotion of elevation. *Prevention and Treatment, 3,* Article 3, posted March 7, 2000. https://pages.stern.nyu.edu/~jhaidt/articles/haidt.2000.the-positive-emotion-of-elevation.pub020.pdf

Hamilton, J. P., Farmer, M., Fogelman, P., & Gotlib, I. H. (2015). Depressive rumination, the Default-Mode Network, and the dark matter of clinical neuroscience. *Biological Psychiatry, 78* (4), 224-230.

Hanh, T. N. (1998). *Interbeing: Fourteen guidelines for engaged Buddhism*. Berkeley, CA: Parallax Press.

Hari, J. (2018). *Lost connections: Uncovering the real causes of depression and the unexpected solutions*. New York, NY: Bloomsbury Publishing.

Havel, V. (1992). *Summer meditations*. P. Wilson (Trans.). New York, NY: Alfred A. Knopf.

Henderson, L. W., Knight, T., & Richardson, B. (2013). An exploration of the well-being benefits of hedonic and eudaimonic behavior. *The Journal of Positive Psychology, 8* (4), 322-336.

Heschel, A. J. (2011). *Essential writings.* S. Heschel (Ed.). New York, NY: Maryknoll.

Hittner, J. B., & Widholm, C. D. (2024). Meta-analysis of the association between gratitude and loneliness. *Applied Psychology, Health, and Well-Being, 16,* 2520-2535.

Hiu, B. P.H., Ng, J.K. C., Berzaghi, E., Cunningham-Amos, L.A., & Kogan, A. (2020). Rewards of kindness? A meta-analysis of the link between prosociality and well-being. *Psychological Bulletin, 146* (12),1084-1116.

Hoge, E.A., Bui, E., Mete, M., Dutton, M. A., Baker, A., & Simon, N. M. (2023). Mindfulness-Based Stress Reduction vs Escitalopram for the treatment of adults with anxiety disorders. *JAMA Psychiatry, 80* (1), 13-21.

Holt-Lunstad, J. (2017). The potential public health relevance of social isolation and loneliness: Prevalence, epidemiology, and risk factors. *Public Policy & Aging Report, 27*(4), 127-130.

Hugh. (2020, January 29). How do trees talk with each other? (Mycorrhizal Network Explained). GetGreenNow. https://get-green-now. com/how-do-trees-talk-with-each-other-mycorrhizal-network explained/#:~:text=Trees%20communicate%20with%20each%20 other%20mainly%20through%20the,together%20into%20a%20 communication%20network%20via%20their%20roots

Huotilainen, M., Rankanen, M., Groth, C., Seitamaa-Hakkarainen, P., & Mäkelä, M. (2018). Why our brains love arts and crafts. *FormAkademisk, 11* (2), Art 1, 1-18. wwwFormAkedemisk.org.

Hurley, D. B., & Kwon, P. (2013). Savoring helps most when you have little: Interaction between savoring the moment and uplifts on positive affect and satisfaction with life. *Journal of Happiness Studies, 14,* 1261-1271.

Hutcherson, C. A., Seppala, E. M., Gross, J. J. (2008). Loving-kindness meditation increases social connectedness. *Emotion, 8* (5), 720-724.

Imperial War Museums. (2025). Voices of the first world war: The Christmas truce. https://www.iwm.org.uk/history/voices-of-the-first-world-war-the-christmas-truce.

Inagaki, T. K., Bryne Haltrom, K. E. Suzuki, S., Jevtic, I., Hornstein, E., Bower, J. E., & Eisenberger, N. I. (2016, May). The neurobiology of giving versus receiving support. *Psychosomatic Medicine, 78* (4), 443-453.

Institute of Noetic Sciences (2024). Experiments. IONS Experiments | Institute of Noetic Sciences.

Jacobs, T. L., Epel, E. S., Blackburn, E. H., Wolkowitz, O. M., Bridwell, D. A., Zanesco, A.P., Aichele, S. R,, Sahdra, B. K., MacLean, K.A., King, B. G., Shaver, P. R., Rosenberg, E. L., Ferrer, E., Wallace, A., & Saron, C. D. (2011). Intensive meditation training, immune cell telomerase activity, and psychological mediators. *Psychoneuroendocrinology, 36,* 664-681.

James, W. (1985). *The varieties of religious experience: A study in human nature.* New York, NY: Penguin Books. Originally published 1902.

Jampolsky, G.G. (2004). *Love is letting go of fear.* Berkeley, CA: Celestial Arts.

Jazaieri, H., Jinpa, G., McGonigal, K., Rosenberg, E., Finkelstein, J., Simon-Thomas, E., Cullen, M., Doty, J., Gross, J., & Goldin, P. (2013). Enhancing compassion: A randomized controlled trial of a Compassion Cultivation Training program. *Journal of Happiness Studies, 14,* 1113-1126.

Jazaieri, H., McGonigal, K., Lee, I. A., Jinpa, T., Doty, J. R., Gross, J. J., & Goldin, P. R. (2018). Altering the trajectory of affect and affect regulation: The impact of compassion training. *Mindfulness, 9* (1), 283-293.

Jevning, R., Wallace, R. K., Beidebach, M. (1988). The physiology of meditation: A review. *Neuroscience and Biobehavioral Reviews, 16,* 415-424.

Jinpa, T. (2015). *A fearless heart: How the courage to be compassionate can transform our lives.* New York, NY: Hudson Street Press.

Jose, P. E., Lim, B. T., Bryant, F. B. (2012). Does savoring increase happiness? A daily diary study. *The Journal of Positive Psychology, 7* (3), 176-187.

Jung, C. G.(1964). *Man and his symbols.* Garden City, NY: Doubleday & Company.

Jung, C.G. (1997). Synchronicity in *Jung on synchronicity and the paranormal.* R. Main (Ed.) (pp. 93-102). Princeton, N.J.: Princeton University Press.

Kabat-Zinn, J. (2023). *Wherever you go, there you are.* New York, NY: Hachette Book Group.

Kabat-Zinn, J. (2012). *Mindfulness for beginners: Reclaiming the present moment—and your life.* Boulder, CO: Sounds True.

Kaimal, G., Ray, K., & Muniz, J. (2016). Reduction of cortisol levels and participants' responses following art-making therapy. *Art Therapy, 33*(2), 74-80.

Kaplan, S. & Berman, M.G. (2013). Directed attention as a common resource for executive functioning and self-regulation. *Perspectives on Psychological Science, 5* (1), 43-57.

Kashdan, T. (2009). *Curious? Discover the missing ingredient to a fulfilling life.* New York, NY: William Morrow.

Kedem-Tahar, E. & Felix-Kellermann, P. (1996). Psychodrama and drama therapy: A comparison. *The Arts in Psychotherapy, 23,* 27-36.

Keltner, D. (2023). *Awe: The new science of everyday wonder and how it can transform your life*. New York, NY: Penguin Press.

Kessler, D. (2019). *Finding meaning: The sixth stage of grief.* New York, NY: Scribner. See also his website, www.Grief.com.

Killingsworth, M.A., & Gilbert, D. (2010,12 November). A wandering mind is an unhappy mind. *Science, 330,* 932.

Kim, N. (2023, September 15). KQED Forum interview with Dr. Jane Goodall. https://www.kqed.org/radio/program/forum. For more about Dr. Goodall's life and work, see https://janegoodall.org/

Kimmerer, R. W. (2015). *Braiding sweetgrass: Indigenous wisdom, scientific knowledge, and the teachings of plants.* Minneapolis, MN: Milkweed Editions.

Klar, M., & Kasser, T. (2009). Some benefits of being an activist: Measuring activism and its role in psychological well-being. *Political Psychology, 30* (5), 755-777.

Kobau, R., Sniezek, J., Zack, M. M., Lucas, R. E., Burns, A. (2010). Well-Being assessment: An evaluation of well-being scales for public health and population estimates of well-being among US adults. *Applied Psychology: Health and Well-Being, 2* (3), 272-297.

Lachman, E. E. & Schiloski, K. A. (2024). The psychosocial anti-inflammatories: Sense of control, purpose in life, and social support in relation to inflammation, functional health and chronic conditions in adulthood. *Journal of Psychosomatic Research, 187,* 111957. https://doi.org/10.1016/jpsychores.2024.111957.

LeDoux, J. (1996). *The emotional brain.* New York, NY: Simon & Schuster.

Levine, P. A. (2008). *Healing trauma: A pioneering program for restoring the wisdom of your body.* Boulder, CO: Sounds True.

Lichtenfeld, S., Elliot, A. J., Maier, M. A., & Pekrun, R. (2012). Fertile green: Green facilitates creative performance. *Personality and Social Psychology Bulletin, 38,* 784-797.

Lickerman, A. (2023, May/June). Levering anticipatory joy. *Psychology Today,* 29.

Luks, A. (2001). *The healing power of doing good: the health and spiritual benefits of helping others.* New York, NY: iUniverse.

Luskin, F. M. (1999). The effect of forgiveness training on psychosocial factors in college age adults. Unpublished dissertation (Stanford University).

Luskin, F. M. (2002). *Forgive for good.* San Francisco, CA: Harper San Francisco.

Lynch, J. (2019). *Win the day.* Camanche, IA: Coaches Choice.

Lyubomirsky, S. (2007). *The how of happiness: A scientific approach to getting the life you want.* New York, NY: Penguin Press.

Lyubomirsky, S., Sheldon, K. M., Schkade, D. (2005). Pursuing happiness: The architecture of sustainable change. *Review of General Psychology, 9,* 111-131.

MacDonald, A.P. (1970). Revised scale for ambiguity tolerance: Reliability and validity. *Psychological Reports, 26,* 791-798.

Madore, K. P., Khazenzon, A. M., Backes, C. W., Jiang, J., Uncapher, M. R., Norcia, A. M., & Wagner, A. D. (2020). Memory failure predicted by attention lapsing and media multitasking. *Nature, 587,* 87-91.

Magsamen, S. & Ross, I. (2023). *Your brain on art.* New York, NY: Random House.

Maharaj, N., Kazanjian, A., & Haney, C.J. (2016). The human-canine bond: A sacred relationship. *Journal of Spirituality in Mental Health, 18*(1), 76-89.

Mallett, S. (2004). Understanding home: A critical review of the literature. *The Sociological Review, 52,* 62-89.

Marsh, J. (2010, August 24). Fred Luskin explains how to forgive. Greater Good Science Center. https://greatergood.berkeley.edu/article/item/fred_luskin_explains_how_to_forgive.

Maslow, A. H. (1971). *The farther reaches of human nature.* New York, NY: Viking Books.

Maté, G. with Maté, D.(2022).*The myth of normal: trauma, illness, & healing in a toxic culture.* New York, NY: Avery.

Mayer, E. L. (2007). *Extraordinary knowing: Science, skepticism, and the inexplicable powers of the human mind.* New York, NY: Bantam.

Mayer, F. S., Frantz, C. M. P., Bruehlman-Senecal, E., & Doliver, K. (2009). Why is nature beneficial? The role of connectedness in nature. *Environment and Behavior, 41,* 607-643.

McCraty, R., Atkinson, M., & Rein, G. (1996). Music enhances the effect of positive emotional states on salivary IgA. *Stress Medicine, 12,* 167-175.

McEwen, B. S. & Lasley, E. N. (2002). *The end of stress as we know it.* Washington, D. C.: Joseph Henry Press.

McGilchrist, I. (2009). *The master and his emissary: The divided brain and the making of the western world.* New Haven, CT: Yale University Press.

McKeown, E., Weir, H., Berridge, E.-J., & Ellis, L. (2016). Art engagement and mental health: Experiences of service users of a community-based arts programme at Tate Modern, London. *Public Health, 130,* 29-35.

McKnight, P. E.& Kashdan, T. B. (2009). Purpose in life as a system that creates and sustains health and well-being: An integrative, testable theory. *Review of General Psychology, 13* (3), 242-251.

McQuillan, J. & Conde, G. (1996). The conditions of flow in reading: Two studies of optimal experience. *Reading Psychology: An International Quarterly, 17,* 109-135.

McTaggart, L. (2008). *The field: The quest for the secret force of the universe.* New York, NY: HarperCollins.

Merton, T. (1948). *The seven storey mountain.* New York, NY: Harcourt Brace & Company.

Mikulincer, M., Shaver, P., Gillath, O., & Nitzberg, R. A. (2005). Attachment, caregiving, and altruism: Boosting attachment security increases compassion and helping. *Journal of Personality and Social Psychology, 89* (5), 817-839.

Miller, L. (2021). *The awakened brain: The new science of spirituality and our quest for an inspired life.* New York, NY: Random House.

Miller, L., Balodis, I. M., McClintock, C. H., Zu, J., Lacadie, C. M., Sinha, R., & Potenza, M. N. (2018). Neural correlates of personalized spiritual experiences. *Cerebral Cortex, 29,* 2331-2338.

Miller, L., Wickramaratne, P., Hao, X., McClintock, C. H., Pan, L., Svob, C., Weissman, M. M. (2021). *Psychiatry Research: Neuroimaging. 315,* 111326.

Miller, T. Q., Smith, T. W., Turner, C. W., Guijarro, M. L., & Hallet, A. J. (1996). A meta-analytic review of research on hostility and physical health. *Psychological Bulletin, 119*(2), 322–348.

Min, J., Rouanet, J., Cadete Martini, A., Nashiro, K., Yoo, H. J., Porat, S., Cho, C., Wan, J., Cole, S. W., Head, E., Nation, D. A., Thayer, J. F., & Mather, M. (2023). Modulating heart rate oscillation affects plasma amyloid beta and tau levels in younger and older adults. *Scientific Reports, 13,* 3967.

Mingyur Rinpoche, Y. (2007). *The joy of living: Unlocking the secrets and science of happiness.* New York, NY: Harmony Books.

Mitchell, E. (2008). *The way of the explorer: An Apollo astronaut's journey through the material and mystical worlds.* Franklin Lakes, NJ: New Page Books.

Morris, T., Manley, D., Northstone, K., & Sabel, C. E. (2017). How do moving and other major life events impact mental health? A longitudinal analysis of UK children. *Health and Place, 46,* 257-266.

Murthy, V. (2020). *Together: The healing power of human connection in a sometimes lonely world.* New York, NY: HarperCollins.

Murthy, V.H. & Chen, A. T. (2020, March 22). The Coronavirus could cause a social recession. *The Atlantic.* https://www.theatlantic.com/ideas/archive/2020/03/america-faces-social-recession/608548/.

Neff, K. (2011). *Self-compassion: Stop beating yourself up and leave insecurity behind.* New York, NY: William Morrow. For more information about self-compassion, see http://www.self-compassion.org/.

Nell, V. (1988). *Lost in a book: The psychology of reading for pleasure.* New Haven, CT: Yale University Press.

Netting, F. E., Wilson, C. C., & New, J. C. (1987). The human-animal bond: Implications for practice. *Social Work, 32* (1), 60-64.

Newberg, A., D'Aquili, E., & Rause, V. (2001). *Why God won't go away.* New York, NY: Ballentine Books.

Nimer, J., & Lundahl, B. (2007). Animal-assisted therapy: A meta-analysis. *Anthrozoös, 20* (3), 225-238.

Nobel Prize in Physics. All Nobel Prizes - NobelPrize.org

Oman, D. & Thoresen, C. (2003). Spiritual modeling: A key to spiritual and religious growth? *The International Journal for the Psychology of Religion. 3,* 149-165.

Oppezzo, M., & Schwartz, D. L. (2014). Give your ideas some legs: The positive effect of walking on creative thinking. *Journal of Experimental Psychology, 40,* 1142-1152.

Osborne, M.T., Radfar, A., Hassan, M. Z. O., Abohashem, S., Oberfeld, B., Patrich, T., Tung, B., Wang, Y., Ishai, A., Scott, J. A., Shin, L. M., Zahi, A. F., Koenen, K. C., Rajagopalan, S., Pitman, R. K., & Tawakol, A., (2020). A neurobiological mechanism linking transportation noise to cardiovascular disease in humans. *European Heart Journal, 41,* 772-782.

Ostafin, B. D., & Proulx, T. (2023). A brief life-purpose intervention reduces trauma-film anxiety and rumination. *The Humanistic Psychologist, 52* (4), 397-406.

Otake, K., Shimai, S., Tanaka-Matsumi, J., Otsui, K, & Fredrickson, B. L. (2006) Happy people become happier through kindness: A counting kindness intervention. *Journal of Happiness Studies, 7,* 361-375.

Panksepp, J. (1998). Attention deficit hyperactivity disorder, psychostimulants, and intolerance of childhood playfulness: A tragedy in the making? *Current Directions in Psychological Science, 7,* 91-98.

Park, B. J., Tsunetsugu, Y., Kasetani, T., Kagawa, T., & Miyasaki, Y. (2010). The physiological effects of *Shinrin-yoku* (taking in the forest atmosphere or forest bathing): Evidence from field experiments in 24 forests across Japan. *Environmental Health Preventive Medicine, 15,* 18-26.

Pennebaker, J. W. (1997). Writing about emotional experiences as a therapeutic process. *Psychological Science, 8,* 162-166.

Pennebaker, J. W., Kiecolt-Glaser, J.K., & Glaser, R. (1988). Disclosure of traumas and immune function: Health implications for psychotherapy. *Journal of Consulting and Clinical Psychology, 56,* 239-245.

Pennebaker, J. W., & Seagal, J. D. (1999). Forming a story: The health benefits of narrative. *Journal of Clinical Psychology, 55,* 1243-1254.

Peterson, C. & Seligman, M. E. P. (2004). *Character strengths and virtues.* Washington, D. C.: American Psychological Association.

Phillips, S. S. (2022, Spring). Tethered by prayer: The spiritual exercises of St. Ignatius Loyola. *Crux, 58* (1), 12.

Piff, P. K., Dietze, P., Feinberg, M., Stancato, D. M, & Keltner, D. (2015). Awe, the small self, and prosocial behavior. *Journal of Personality and Social Psychology, 108,* 883-899.

Plonka, N., McCraty, R., van der Westhuyzen, L., & Edwards, S. D. (2023). Global consciousness project 2.0: A first look. *Dialogo, 10* (1), 37-49.

Pöllänen, S. (2006). Crafts as a way to functional mental health. In A-L. Rauma, S. Pöllänen, & P. Seitamaa-Hakkarainen. (Eds.). *Human Perspectives on Sustainable Future* (pp. 128-134). New York, NY: Reuters.

Popova, M. (2016). Einstein on widening our circles of compassion. The Marginalian. Einstein's letter written 1950.

Post, S. G. (2011). It's good to be good: 2011 5th annual scientific report on health, happiness, and helping others. *The International Journal of Person-Centered Medicine, 1* (4), 814-829.

Proyer, R. Y., Brauer, K., Gander, F., & Chick, G. (2021). Can playfulness be stimulated? A randomized placebo-controlled online playfulness intervention study on effects on trait playfulness, well-being, and depression. *Applied Psychology Health and Well-Being, 13* (1), 129-151.

Rein, G., Atkinson, M., & McCraty, R. (1995). The physiological and psychological effects of compassion and anger. *Journal of Advancement in Medicine. 8* (2), 87-105.

Robinson, J. P. & Godbey, G. (2005). Busyness as usual. *Social Research, 72* (2), 407-427.

Root-Bernstein, R., Allen, L, Bhadula, R., Fast, J., Hosey, C., Kremkow, B., Lapp, J., Lonc, K., Pawelec, K., Podufaly, A., Russ, C., Tennant, L., Vrtis, E., & Weinlander, S. (2008). Arts foster scientific success: Avocations of Nobel, National Academy, Royal Society, and Sigma Xi members. *Journal of Psychology of Science and Technology, 1* (3), 51-63.

Rosenkranz, M. A., Lutz, A., Perlman, D. M., Bachhuber, D.R.W., Schuyler, B., MacCoon, D., & Davidson, R.J. (2026). Reduced stress and inflammatory responsiveness in experienced meditators compared to a matched healthy control group. *Psychoneuroendocrinology,68,* 117-125.

Rozin, P., & Royzman, E. B. (2001). Negativity bias, negativity dominance, and contagion. *Personality and Social Psychology Review, 5,* 296-320.

Ryan, R. M., Weinstein, N., Bernstein, J., Brown, K. W., Mistretta, L., & Gagne, M. (2010). Vitalizing effects of being outdoors and in nature. *Journal of Environmental Psychology, 30,* 159-168.

Ryff, C. D. (1989). Happiness is everything, or is it? Explorations on the meaning of psychological well-being. *Journal of Personality and Social Psychology, 57* (6), 1069-1081.

Sagan, C. (1980). *Cosmos.* New York, NY: Random House.

Salzberg, S. (1995). *Loving-Kindness: The revolutionary art of happiness.* Boston, MA: Shambhala.

Samuel, K. (2022). *Belonging: Finding connection in an age of isolation.* New York, NY: Abrams Press.

Sanchez-Villegas, A., Ara, I., Guillen-Grima, F., Bes-Rastrollo, M., Varo-Cenarruzabeitia, J. J., & Martinez-Gonzalez, M. A. (2008). Physical activity, sedentary index, and mental disorders in the SUN cohort study. *Medicine & Science in Sports & Exercise, 40 (5),* 1-8.

Sato, I., Jose, P. E., & Conner, T. S. (2018). Savoring mediates the effect of nature on positive affect. *International Journal of Wellbeing, 8*(1). https://www.internationaljournalofwellbeing.org/index.php/ijow/article/view/621

Savage, B.M., Lujan, H. I., Thipparthi, R. R., & DeCarlo, S. E. (2017). Humor, laughter, learning, and health! A brief review. *Advances in Physiology Education, 41,* 341-347.

Schaper, E. (1968, April). Aristotle's catharsis and aesthetic pleasure. *The Philosophical Quarterly, 18* (71), 131-143.

Schubert, C. (2012, May). Pursuing happiness. *Kyklos, 65* (2), 245-261.

Schwartz, J.M. (1998). Neuroanatomical aspects of cognitive-behavioural therapy response in obsessive-compulsive disorder: An evolving perspective on brain and behavior. *British Journal of Psychiatry, 173, Suppl 35,* 38-44.

Schwerwitz, L., Graham, E., Grandits, G., Buehler, J., Billings, J. (1986). Self-involvement and coronary heart disease incidence in the multiple risk factor intervention trial. *Psychosomatic Medicine, 48* (3/4), 187-199.

Seligman, M. E. P. (2002). *Authentic Happiness.* New York, NY: Free Press.

Seligman, M. E. P., Steen, T. A., Park, N, & Peterson, C. (2005). Positive psychology progress: Empirical validation of interventions. *American Psychologist, 60,* 410-421.

Shakespeare, W. (1997). *The Norton Shakespeare.* S. Greenblatt (Ed.). New York, NY: W. W. Norton & Company. Plays originally published in 1623.

Shapiro, S.L., & Carlson, L. E.(2009). *The art and science of mindfulness.* Washington, D.C.: American Psychological Association.

Sheldrake, R. (2009). *Morphic resonance.* Rochester, VT: Park Street Press.

Sheldrake, R. (2011). *Dogs that know when their owners are coming home: And other unexplained powers of animals.* New York, NY: Three Rivers Press.

Sheldrake, R. (2017). *Science and spiritual practices.* Berkeley, CA: Counterpoint.

Silcox, D. Castillo, Y.A., Reed, B. J. (2014). The human animal bond: Applications for rehabilitation professionals. *Journal of Applied Rehabilitation Counseling, 45* (3), 27-37.

Singer, T., & Klimecki, O. M. (2014). Empathy and compassion. *Current Biology, 24* (18), R875-R878.

Snyder, C. R. (1994). *Making hope happen.* New York, NY: Free Press.

Soga, M., Gaston, K. J., & Yamaura, Y. (2017). Gardening is beneficial for health: A meta analysis. *Preventive medicine reports, 5,* 92-99.

Spivak, B., & Saunders, P. A. (2020). *Antidote to violence: Evaluating the evidence.* Alresford, Hampshire, UK: Changemakers Books.

Stapleton, L. (Ed.). (1960). *H.D. Thoreau: A writer's journal.* New York, NY: Dover Publications, Inc.

Stellar, J. E., John-Henderson, N., Anderson, C. L., Gordon, A. M., McNeil, G. D., & Keltner, D. (2015). Positive affect and markers of inflammation: Discrete positive emotions predict lower levels of inflammatory cytokines. *Emotion, 15,* 129-133. http://dx.doi.org/10.1037/emo0000033.

Strack, F., Martin, L. L., & Stepper, S. (1988). Inhibiting and facilitating conditions of the human smile: A nonobtrusive test of the facial feedback hypothesis. *Journal of Personality and Social Psychology, 54* (5), 768-777.

Taylor, J. B. (2021). *Whole brain living: The anatomy of choice and the four characters that drive our life.* Carlsbad, CA: Hay House.

Taylor, J. M., & Rowe, B. J. (2012). The "Mozart effect" and the mathematical connection. *Journal of College Reading and Learning, 42,* 51-66.

Taylor, S. (2022). *Disconnected: The roots of human cruelty and how connection can heal the world.* Alresford, UK: John Hunt Publishing.

Taylor, S. (2023, September/October). The Mind of a hero. *Psychology Today,* 42-45.

Tedeschi, R. G., & Calhoun, L. G. (2004). Posttraumatic growth: Conceptual foundations and empirical evidence. *Psychological Inquiry, 15* (1), 1-18.

Tennen, H., & Affleck, G. (1990). Blaming others for threatening events. *Psychological Bulletin, 108* (2), 209–232.

Teoh, S. L., Letchumanan, V., & Lee, L. H. (2021, February 25). Can mindfulness help to alleviate loneliness? A systematic review and meta-analysis. *Frontiers in Psychology, 12,* 633319.

Thoreau, H.D. (1960). *Walden.* New York, NY: New American Library. Originally published in 1854.

Thorp, A. A., Owen, N., Neuhaus, M., & Dunstan, D. W. (2011). Sedentary behaviors and subsequent health outcomes in adults: A systematic review of longitudinal studies, 1996-2011. *American Journal of Preventive Medicine, 41,* 207-215.

Townsend, M. (2006). Feel blue? Touch green! Participation in forest/ woodland management as a treatment for depression. *Urban Forestry & Urban Greening, 5,* 111-120.

Traherne, T. (1960). *Centuries.* Oxford, UK: Clarendon Press. Originally published 1908.

Twenge, J. M., Spitzberg, B. H., Campbell, W. K. (2019). Less in-person social interaction with peers among U.S. adolescents in the 21st century and links to loneliness. *Journal of Social and Personal Relationships. 20* (10), 1-22.

Ulrich, R. S. (1984). View through a window may influence recovery from surgery. *Science, 224,* 420-421.

Ulrich, R. S., Simons, R. F., Losito, B. D., Fiorito, E, Miles, M. A., & Zelson, M. (1991). Stress recovery during exposure to natural and urban environments. *Journal of Environmental Psychology, 11,* 201-230.

Underhill, E. (1915). *Practical mysticism.* New York, NY: E. P. Dutton & Co.

Van Cappellen, P. Ladd, K. L., Cassidy, S., Edwards, M. E., & Fredrickson, B. L. (2022). Bodily feedback: Expansive and upward posture facilitates the experience of positive affect. *Cognition and Emotion, 36* (7), 1327-1342.

van der Kolk, B. (2015). *The body keeps the score: Brain, mind, and body in the healing of trauma.* New York, NY: Penguin Putnam,

Van Lith, T., Schofield, M. J., & Fenner, P. (2013). Identifying the evidence-base for art-based practices and their potential benefit for mental health recovery: A critical review. *Disability & Rehabilitation, 35,* 1309-1323.

Vieten, C., Amorok, T., Schlitz, M. M. (2006). I to we: The role of consciousness transformation in compassion and altruism. *Zygon, 41* (4), 915-931.

Wahbeh, H., Fry, N., Speirn, P., Hrnjic, L., Ancel, E., & Niebauer, E. (2022). Qualitative analysis of first-person accounts of noetic experiences. *F1000Research, 10* (497), 1-30.

Wahbeh, H., Radin, E., Mossbridge, J., Vieten, C., & Delorme, A. (2018, September/October). Exceptional experiences reported by scientists and engineers. *Explore, 14* (5), 329-341.

Wahbeh, H., Sagher, A., Back, W., Pundhit, P., & Tavris, F. (2018). A systematic review of transcendent states across meditative and contemplative traditions. *Explore, 14* (1), 19-35.

Waldinger, R., & Schulz, M. (2023). *The good life: Lessons from the world's longest scientific study of happiness.* New York, NY: Simon & Schuster.

Watkins, P. C., Cruz, L., Holben, H., & Kolts, R. L. (2008). Taking care of business? Grateful processing of unpleasant memories. *The Journal of Positive Psychology, 3* (2), 87-99.

Watkins, P., Emmons, R., Davis, D., & Frederick, M. (2024). Thanks be to God: Divine gratitude and its relationship to well-being. *Religions, 15,* 1246. https://doi.org/10.3390/rel51011246.

Weinstein, D., Launay, J., Pearce, E., Dunbar, R. I. M., & Stewart, L. (2016). Singing and social bonding: changes in connectivity and pain threshold as a function of group size. *Evolution and Human Behavior, 37,* 152-158.

Weng, H. Y., Fox, A.S., Shackman, A.J., Stodola, D.E., Caldwell, J. Z.K., Olson M.C., Rogers, G.M., & Davidson, R. J. (2013). Compassion training alters altruism and neural responses to suffering. *Psychological Science, 24* (7), 1171-1180.

Werner, E. E. & Smith, R. S. (1992). *Overcoming the odds; High risk children from birth to adulthood.* Ithaca, NY: Cornell University Press.

Williams, M., Teasdale, J., Segal, Z., Kabat-Zinn, J. (2007). *The mindful way through depression*. New York, NY: Guilford Press.

Winston, J. (2006). Beauty, goodness and education: the arts beyond utility. *Journal of Moral Education, 35,* 285-300.

Woodward, J. & Sikes, P. L. (2015). The creative thinking ability of musicians and nonmusicians. *Psychology of Aesthetics, Creativity, and the Arts, 4,* 75-80.

World Health Organization. (2022, March 2). COVID-19 pandemic triggers 25% increase in prevalence of anxiety and depression worldwide https://www.who.int/news/item/02-03-2022-covid-19-pandemic-triggers-25-increase-in-prevalence-of-anxiety-and-depression-worldwide.

World Health Organization. (2024, May 21). World health statistics 2024: monitoring health for the SDGs, sustainable development goals https://www.who.int/publications/i/item/9789240094703.

Worthington, E. L., & Scherer, M. (2004). Forgiveness is an emotion-focused coping strategy that can reduce health risks and promote resilience: theory, review, and hypotheses. *Psychology & Health, 19* (3), 385-405.

Yim, J. (2016). Therapeutic benefits of laughter in mental health: A theoretical review. *Tohoku Journal of Experimental Medicine, 239,* 243-249.

Yount, R., Ritchie, E. C., St. Laurent, M., Chumley, P., & Olmert, M. D. (2013). The role of service dog training in the treatment of combat-related PTSD. *Psychiatric Annals, 43* (6), 292-295.

Zaccaro, A., Piarulli, A, Laurino, M, Garbella, E., Menicucci, D., Neri, B., & Gemignani, A. (2018). How breath-control can change your life: A systematic review on psycho-physiological correlates of slow breathing. *Frontiers in Human Neuroscience, 12,* 353. Doi: 10.3389/fnhum.2018.00353.

Zimmerman, J., Borckmeyer, T., Hunn, M., Schauenburg, H., & Wolf, M.(2017). First-person pronoun use in spoken language as a predictor of future depressive symptoms: Preliminary evidence from a clinical sample of depressed patients. *Clinical Psychology and Psychotherapy,* *24,* 384-391

Acknowledgements

Years ago, Czech poet, playwright, and political leader Vaclav Havel (1991) described home as a multidimensional experience in which we're surrounded by concentric circles of connection from our families and close friends to our neighborhoods, towns, workplaces, countries, and the world in which we live.

While writing this book, I've developed a deep appreciation of Havel's vision, feeling a sense of home and connection with my loved ones, friends, neighborhood, community, country, and our beautiful natural world.

I'm grateful to have shared my life with my loving partner, Bob Numan. For years, I've felt a sense of home at my university, in my neighborhood and the town where I live. I gratefully acknowledge my connections with the following people who've supported my life and work on this book in their own unique ways.

My Circle of Education

I'm grateful for the many mentors, guides, fellow students, and students who've shared the path of education with me. To my high school friends, Anne Findlay Johnson and Rudi Kasic Weissinger; my college friends from UC Riverside including Carol Daeley, Ann Kelsey, Brad Parker, and Pat Stubblefield; my grad school friends from UCLA including Liahna Armstrong, Janette Lewis, Pat Patrick as well as James Patrick and Julie Schlax Patrick; my professors and mentors, Paul Jorgensen and Stanley Stewart; my grad school professors and colleagues in the Counseling Psychology Program at Santa Clara University including David Feldman, Dale Larson, and Shauna Shapiro; and my friends and colleagues at Santa Clara University, past and present, including Ahmed Amer, Bill Barker, Simone Billings, Julie Chang, Jane Curry, Jim Degnan, Don Dodson, Marilyn Edelstein, Eileen Elrod, Barb Fraser, Lucia and Jack Gilbert, Barbara Gold, Jill Goodman Gould, Joe Grassi, Mary Hegland, Diane Jonte-Pace, Tracey Kahan, Barbara Kelley, Chris Lievestro, Carolyn Mitchell, Catherine Montfort, Claudia Monpere, Elizabeth Moran, Tim Myers, Fred Parrella, William Rewak, SJ, Ted Rynes, SJ, Bill Sullivan, Nancy Unger, Juan Velasco, Cory Wade, Fred White, Ann Wittman, and Alex Zecevic; my friends and colleagues in the Osher Lifelong Learning Program; and my wonderful students including Sammi Bennett, Jeff Capaccio, Kevin Carroll, Sachit Egan, Christina Fialho, Isabel Filiz, Cece Garrison, Lisa Marie Lombardi, Ryan Nazari, Faolan Sugarman-Lash, and many others.

My Positive Psychology Circle

For their leading-edge research, I'm grateful to Christopher Peterson, Rhett Diessner, Carol Dweck, Barbara Fredrickson, Dacher Keltner, Martin Seligman, and my Santa Clara University counseling psychology colleagues; and to Tom Plante and the Institute of Applied Spirituality for ongoing research on positive psychology and spirituality. For bringing positive psychology into coaching, I'm grateful to my friends and colleagues at MentorCoach including Ben Dean, Sunny Bain, Ann Durand, and Gayle Scroggs. For her creative coaching for parents, I'm grateful to Gloria DeGaetano, founder of the Parent Coaching Institute, and for her leadership in sharing the power of hope to heal our lives, I'm grateful to Kathryn Goetzke. For their innovative work extending the power of positive psychology to many professions throughout the world, I'm grateful to Reece Coker, founder and president, and Claire Higgins, chief operating officer, of the Positive Psychology Guild in the UK.

My Community Support Circle

I am grateful to Joe Gorelick, Debbie Hanson, Sharon Robinson, Eve Solis, Brenda Tierney, Robin Welch, Erna Wenus, and Carol Zimbelman, and to Doctors Karen Kunzel, Shari Johnson, Michelle Mak-Fung, Gianna O'Connor, David Reed, Megan Rivera, Indira Singh, and Allen Vu, for their support in health and healing for my loved ones and me. For their professional support in many areas, I am grateful to Kyle Ferguson, Amy Gaw, Michael Lonich, Daniel Lopretta, Sarada Majumdar, Jonathan Rafael, and Cliff Silva.

My Spiritual Circle.

For the light of inspiration, I am grateful to the Blue Mountain Center of Meditation, the HeartMath Institute, to Gen Farrow and Ilene Berns-Zare; to Hazel Donaldson, Maud Gleason, Carolyn Irish, Thea Sawyer, Tom Sawyer, Bob Simmons, Sandhya Viswanathan, and Vishy Viswanathan of the Los Gatos Satsang; to Rabbi Hugh Seid-Valencia, Gerri Finkelstein-Lurya, and Mary Ann Welch at the APJCC; to Father Angelo David and the members of St. Mary's Church; and to nature's green cathedral and this beautiful planet we call home.

Family and Friendship Circle

I am grateful to my father, Colonel Frank H. Dreher, whose courage, kindness, and integrity made him a role model for my life, to my mother Mary Ann Dreher and brother Frank Dreher, Jr., who taught me a lot; to my dear cousins Norma MacCaskey and Jerry Garrison; to Bob's family, Michael Numan, Marilyn Numan, Bobbi Numan Erd, Ron Erd, Todd Numan, Marjorie Numan, Zachary Numan, Ethan Numan, and my dear niece Suzy Numan; my neighbors Cathy and Diane Barrera; and my chosen family of friends who continue to inspire me including Rose Marie Beebe and Bob Senkewicz, Holly Christensen, Tina Clare, Laura Ellingson, MaryLinda Kamas, Will Schneider and Kaya Johnson, Tom Schneider, Cristina Schneider, Carl Vitale, and Veronica Vitale, who has included me in the loving embrace of her family.

My Writing Circle

For their ongoing inspiration, insights, and support, I am grateful to the Authors Guild; Stephanie Chandler and the Nonfiction Authors Association; and to my fellow authors Charlie Birney, Michelle Chappel, Carol Flinders, Carolyn Grassi, Ron Hanson, Rick Herrick, Frances Moore Lappé, Sunny

Lockwood, Ed Mayes, Francis Pring-Mill, and Katherine Woodall for sharing the ongoing adventure of writing with me.

For sharing their stories and information from interviews included in this book, my thanks to James R. Doty, Loren Ellis, Kathryn Goetzke, Jerry Lynch, and Susan Phillips. I am grateful to my agent, Elise Capron, and to Sandy Dijkstra and the staff at the Sandra Dijkstra Literary Agency; to my editor at MSI Press, Betty Lou Leaver, to Opeyemi Ikuborije for cover design and layout, and to Jacquelyn Johnson and Franklin Uweke for promotional support.

And finally, to you who are reading this book. May you discover more loving comfort, peace, and renewal in your own expanding circles of connection.

I wish you joy on the journey.

Index

www.ingramcontent.com/pod-product-compliance
Lightning Source LLC
Chambersburg PA
CBHW070557100426
42744CB00006B/321